Excel Power Suite
Business Intelligence Clinic
Create and Learn

Roger F Silva

Copyright © 2026 by Roger F. Silva – Create and Learn

No part of this publication may be reproduced, stored, transmitted, or distributed in any form or by any means—electronic, mechanical, photocopying, recording, scanning, or otherwise—without the prior written permission of the publisher, except for brief quotations used in reviews or other non-commercial uses permitted by applicable copyright laws.

This book, including any accompanying files, downloads, links, and references, is provided for educational and informational purposes only. Although every effort has been made to ensure accuracy and up-to-date guidance at the time of publication, software features, interfaces, licensing, and online services may change without notice. The author and publisher make no warranties, express or implied, and accept no responsibility for any loss, damages, or liabilities resulting from the use of the information, files, or software mentioned in this material.

Permission Requests

For permissions and licensing requests, please contact:

Roger F. Silva

contact.createandlearn@gmail.com

createandlearn.net

www.linkedin.com/in/roger-f-silva

Edition: 2026 (Revised)

ISBN: 9781094631837

Contents

About this book vii

MS Windows and Excel System Requirements viii

Important to know x

Introduction 1

Get Started 3

    1.   Business Intelligence and Excel "Power Suite" 3

    2.   Power Query (Get & Transform) 4

    3.   Where are Power Query (Get & Transform) and Power Pivot? 5

    4.   The Business Intelligence Clinic Dataset 7

Get Data 8

Data Model 40

    5.   Measures 49

Creating (Power) PivotCharts 51

    6.   Clustered Columnn 51

    7.   Doughnut Chart 66

    8.   Line Chart 75

    9.   Stacked Bar 85

Creating (Power) Pivot Tables 97

    10. PivotTable Revenue By Product Line 97

    11. PivotTable Revenue 108

    12. PivotTable Gross Margin 119

    13. PivotTable Countries 122

Linking Data 132

Creating Special Visuals 140

    14. Treemap 140

    15. Field Map 144

Slicer and Timeline 149

Setup Printing 161

Sharing online 167

Next Steps 173

Final words 175

v

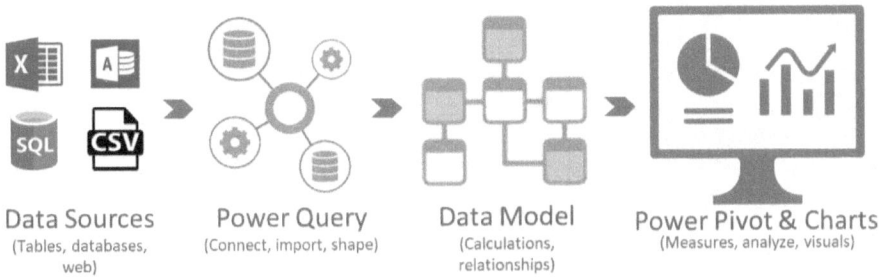

For more **Create and Learn** books, visit
www.createandlearn.net

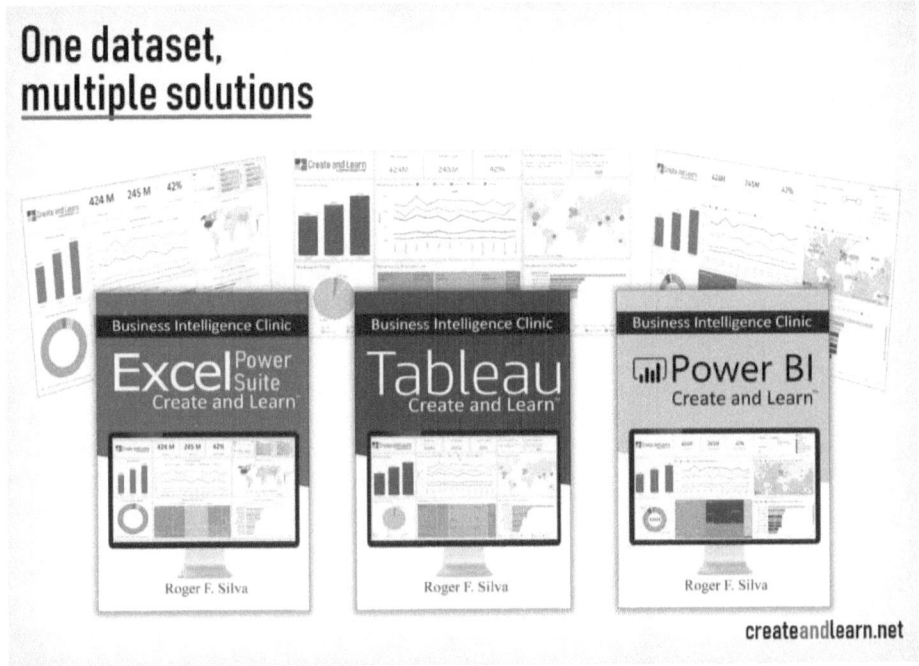

www.createandlearn.net

About this book

In the Business Intelligence Clinic series, every book will use a specific Business Intelligence solution to create, step-by-step, a Global **Sales Dashboard**, allowing the reader to learn how to use multiple tools and methods. In this book, **Excel Power Suite – Business Intelligence Clinic**, the main points touched are:

1. Use Excel Power Suite (Power Query, Data Model, and Power Pivot).
2. Manipulate images, objects, and charts.
3. Create custom calculations using DAX (Data Analysis Expressions).
4. Create and configure Timelines.
5. Create and configure Slicers.
6. Create and edit Power Pivots and Power Charts.
7. Create special charts from formulas linked to Power Pivot.
8. Advanced chart formatting.
9. Share online and set up printing.

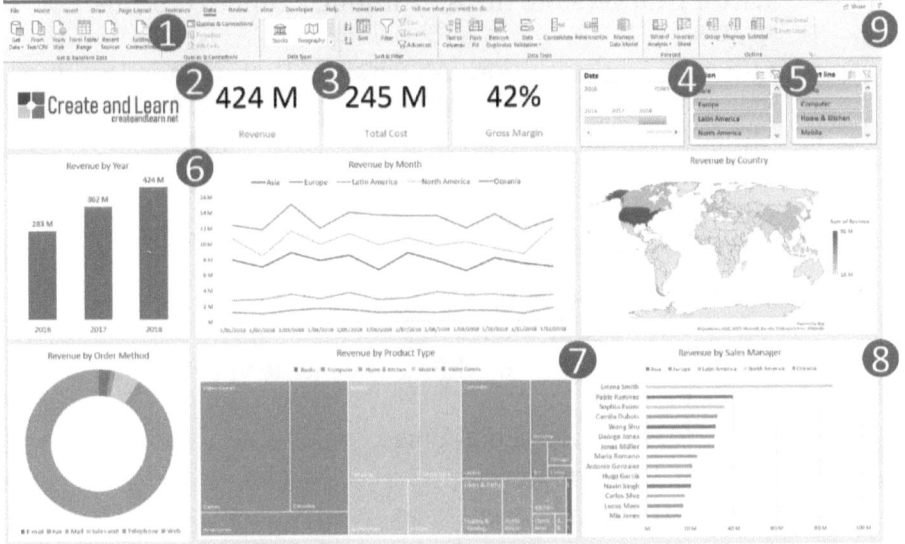

www.createandlearn.net

MS Windows and Excel System Requirements

To get the most out of this book, you must have an Excel version with **Power Query (Get & Transform)** and **PowerPivot**. If you don't have one, you can download a **one-month free trial** and use the trial version to follow this book:

If you need the trial version, you can download it in the Microsoft website or try this link: https://products.office.com/en-us/try

You will need:

1. Windows operating system: **Windows** 7 or later (Windows 10/11 recommended).
2. One of the following Microsoft Excel on the **Windows** operating system:
    - Excel Microsoft 365 (64-bit) recommended.
    - Latest trial version: https://products.office.com/en-us/try
    - Office 365 subscription- All versions that include Desktop versions of Excel for Windows
    - Office Professional 2021
    - Office Home & Business 2021
    - Office Home & Student 2021
    - Office Professional 2019
    - Office Home & Business 2019
    - Office Home & Student 2019
    - Office 2016 Professional Plus (available via volume licensing only)
    - Office 2013 Professional Plus
    - Excel 2013 standalone
    - Excel 2016 standalone

The Microsoft Excel version used in this book is the **Microsoft 365 2026.**

If you have questions about compatibility, go to the Microsoft page or Google **Where is Power Pivot?**

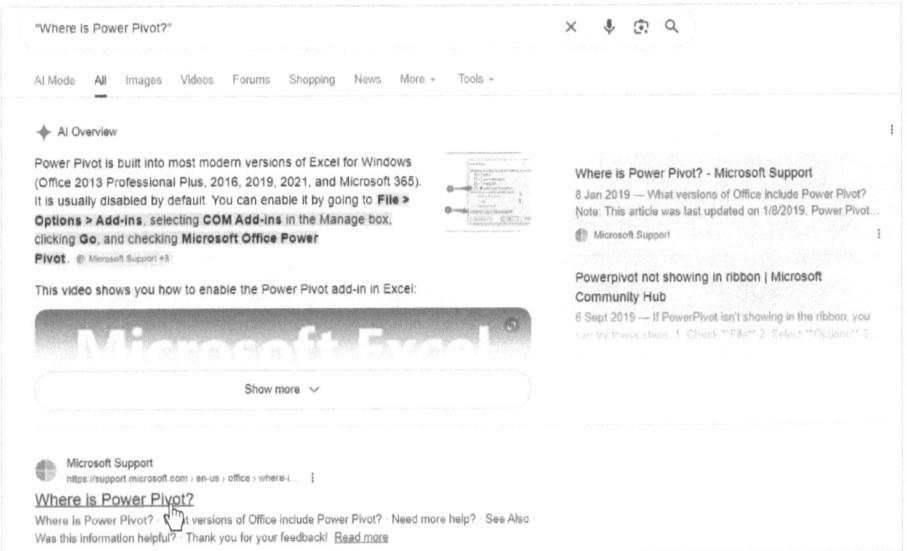

www.createandlearn.net

Important to know

A few points are essential to have in mind once you start to work through this book:

a. Power Query and Power Pivot are powerful tools from Excel, and they demand good processing capability and work better in a 64-bit version.
b. Here is the version that I used in this book: Microsoft® Excel® for Microsoft 365 MSO (Version 2604 Build 16.0.19929.20086) 64-bit
c. Save your files! Although I had no problem during this book's creation, saving your files as you proceed is recommended.
d. Microsoft is constantly updating Microsoft Excel. Although icons or places can change, you should be good to use this book if you have a compatible version.

Introduction

Dear reader,

The **Business Intelligence Clinic** series will help you explore various Business Intelligence (BI) solutions.

Each book covers a different BI tool, and you will follow step-by-step instructions to create a professional sales dashboard using the same friendly dataset. The BI Clinic series will help you compare different business intelligence tools, learn the basics, and select the best for your project, company, customers, or personal needs.

In this Create and Learn book, **Excel Power Suite – Business Intelligence Clinic**, you will review important Microsoft Excel topics and its Power Suite (Power Query, Data Model, and Power Pivot), a powerful Business Intelligence toolset. You will learn to **get data** from external sources, **model** your data, work with **visuals and reports**, create a s**ales dashboard**, and s**hare** your work with others.

We will not go into deep theories as this book's purpose and all Create and Learn material is to make the most of your time and learn by doing.

I hope this book will help you start your journey in the Business Intelligence world and give you the right tools to build professional reports and dashboards using Microsoft Excel and its Power Suite.

You can find more here https://www.createandlearn.net/excelbi

Thank you for creating and learning.

Roger F. Silva

rogerfsilva1@gmail.com

createandlearn.net

www.linkedin.com/in/roger-f-silva

Chapter 1
Get Started

1. Business Intelligence and Excel "Power Suite"

The primary goal of Business Intelligence is to help people and companies make better decisions. According to Wikipedia, business intelligence is a set of methodologies, processes, architectures, and technologies that transform raw data into meaningful and useful information to enable more effective strategic, tactical, and operational insights and decision-making.

Until recently, Business Intelligence solutions were aimed at Enterprise-level BI, with complex and costly products, and most of it was done by IT professionals.

Nowadays, you can find various BI solutions, and Excel Power Suite can help immensely. These solutions allow salespeople, analysts, managers, and professionals to get, model, create visualizations and share data.

Power Query for Excel is a data connection technology that allows users to get data from multiple sources and combine and refine it. Once the data is available, the user can use the **Data Model** and **PowerPivot** to create data models, set relationships, and create calculations.

This powerful combination of Power Query, Data Model, and PowerPivot is called **Excel "Power Suite,"** and it makes Excel a viable choice as a Business Intelligence tool, allowing users to **get** millions of rows of data,

model the data, build **relationships**, create custom **calculations**, create **reports**, dashboards, and visualizations.

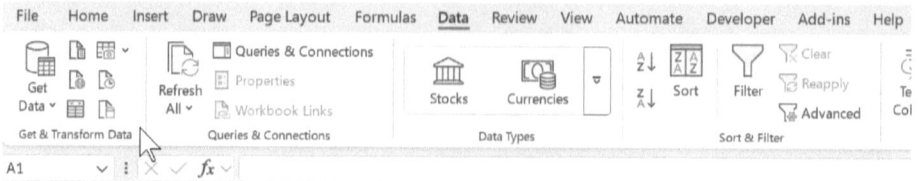

2. Power Query (Get & Transform)

Power Query can be downloaded for Excel 2010 and 2013, and since the Excel 2016 version, the name Power Query has changed to **Get & Transform**.

Most users still prefer the name **Power Query** once the previous add-in is widespread worldwide and still part of Power BI software. So, don't worry if you see both names, Power Query and Get & Transform, used across the web and in this book.

3.   Where are Power Query (Get & Transform) and Power Pivot?

In the recent versions, Power Query was renamed to **Get & Transform**, and it is already installed in the **Data** tab.

Power Pivot needs to be activated most of the time. Follow the instructions below if you cannot see the **Power Pivot** tab.

1. Click on the File tab.

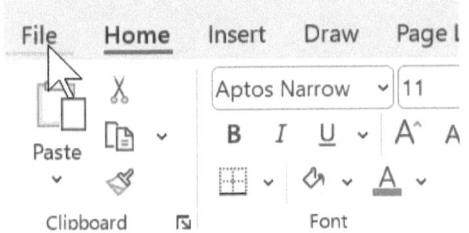

2. Select Options.

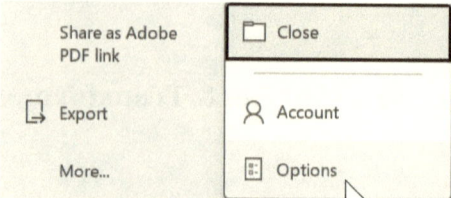

3. Go to **Add-ins**, **Manage**, select **COM Add-ins,** and click on **Go...**

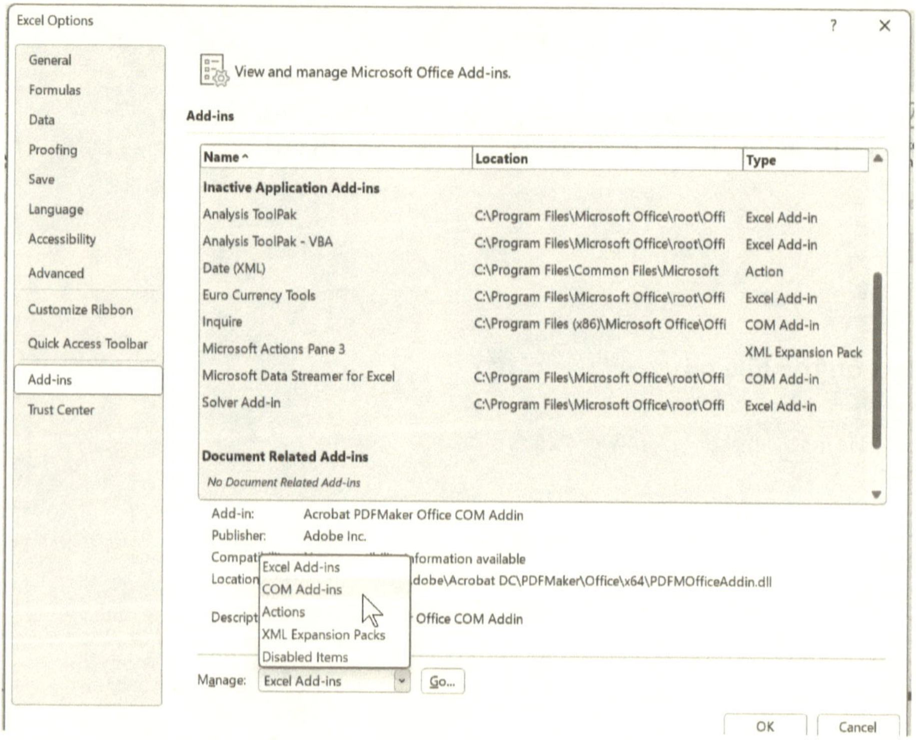

Get Started

4. Make sure you have checked the options **Power Pivot for Excel**. Then click **OK**. If you have installed other versions of the Power Pivot add-in, those versions are also in the COM Add-ins list. Be sure to select the Power Pivot add-in for Excel. You may need to close and open Excel again.

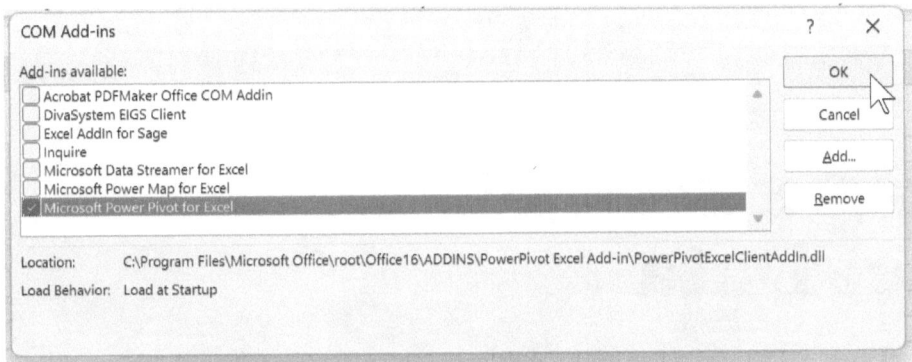

5. The ribbon now has a Power Pivot tab.

4. The Business Intelligence Clinic Dataset

The Business Intelligence Clinic dataset is a friendly, easy-to-read set of four tables containing high-level sales information from a fictitious company. They will be used in every BI Clinic book.

These are the tables you will find:

Sales: Contains the main sales data in a three-year range.

Region: Contains countries and regions where the company operates.

SalesManager: Contains the sales manager's names by country.

Dates: Contains the dates and group of dates.

www.createandlearn.net

Chapter 2
Get Data

With Microsoft Excel, you can connect different data sources and types. You can use basic sources such as CSV files, spreadsheets, and Databases until online services such as Azure.

1. Visit the address **createandlearn.net/bifiles** and download the **SalesData.xlsx** . This file contains the data you will use to create the Sales Dashboard.

Webpage Download Option

Book material:

Right-click the image and click on **Save image as**

SalesData.xlsx

Get Data

2. If it asks for a **password**, type: **bifiles**

3. Open Microsoft Excel, go to **New** and click on **Blank workbook**.

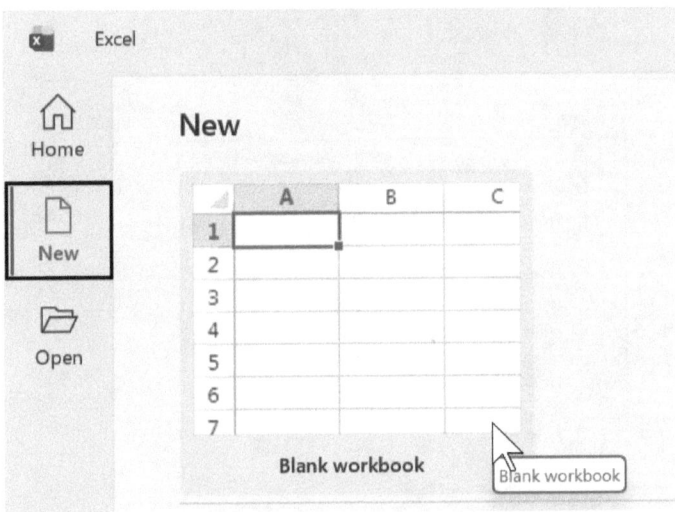

4. Go to the **Data** tab, **Get Data**, **From file**, and select **From Workbook**.

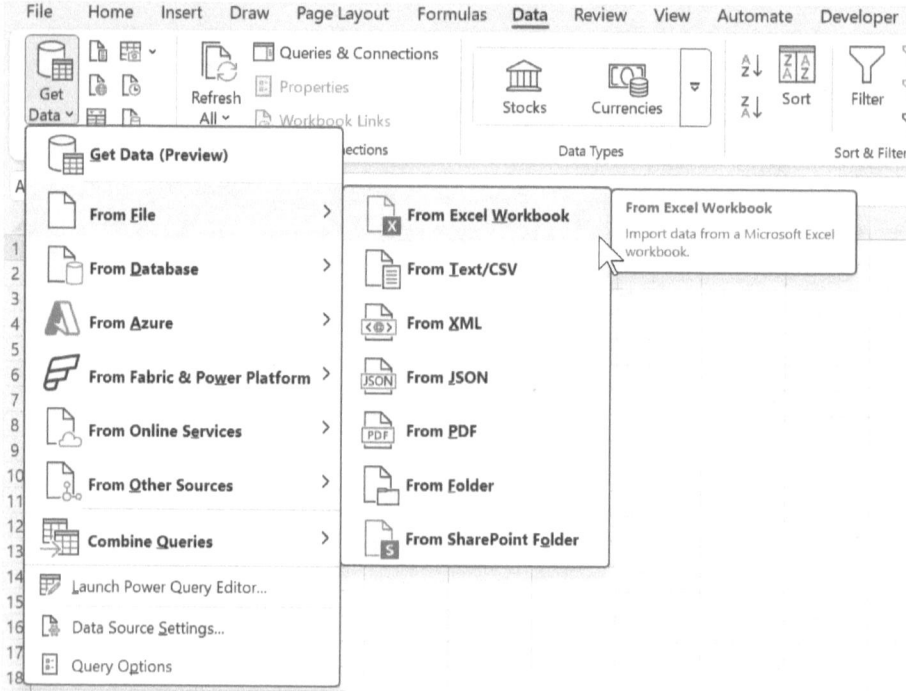

5. Select the file **SalesData.xlsx** saved from the website and click **Import**.

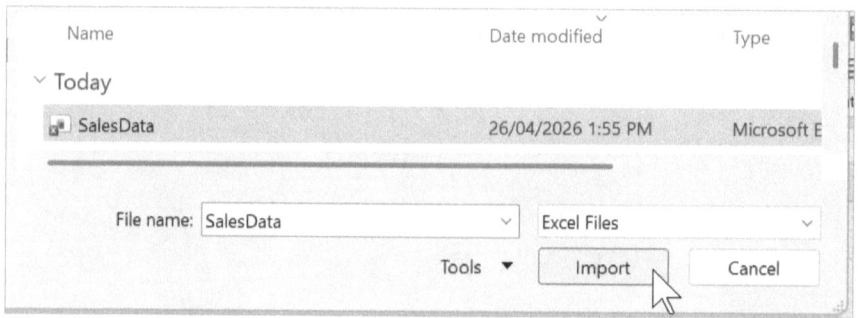

Get Data

6. The Navigator view will show the options to be loaded in the spreadsheet.

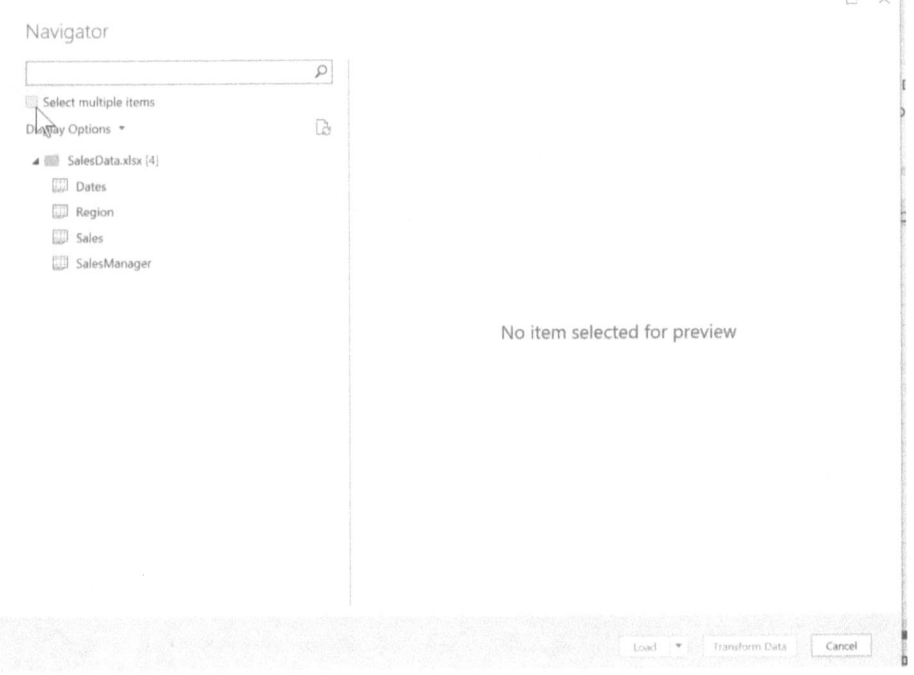

7. Check the box **Select multiple items**. Then, select the four tables available: **Dates**, **Region**, **Sales**, and **Sales Manager**.

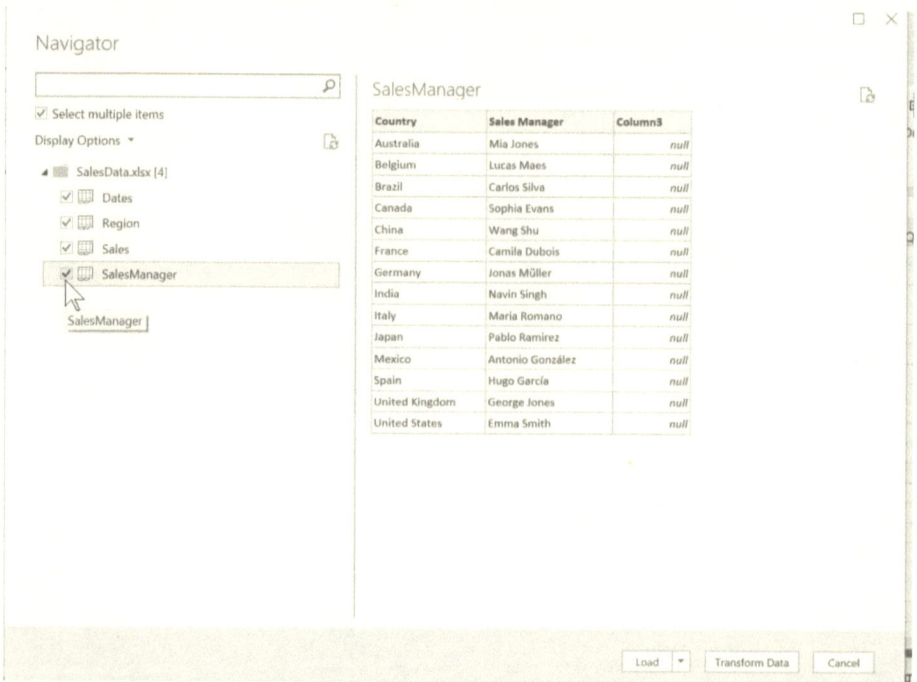

8. Click on the Load **Arrow** to show more options, and select **Load To...** Note: If we choose the **Load** option, the data will be loaded directly in the spreadsheet. However, we need to load the tables in the **data model** to access them whenever required. We will see how it works further.

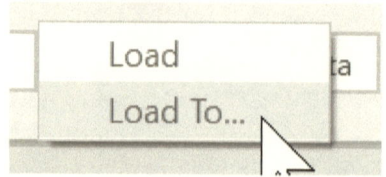

Get Data

9. The **Import Data** window will appear. Select **Only Create Connection**, and check the box **Add this data to the Data Model**. Then, click **OK**.

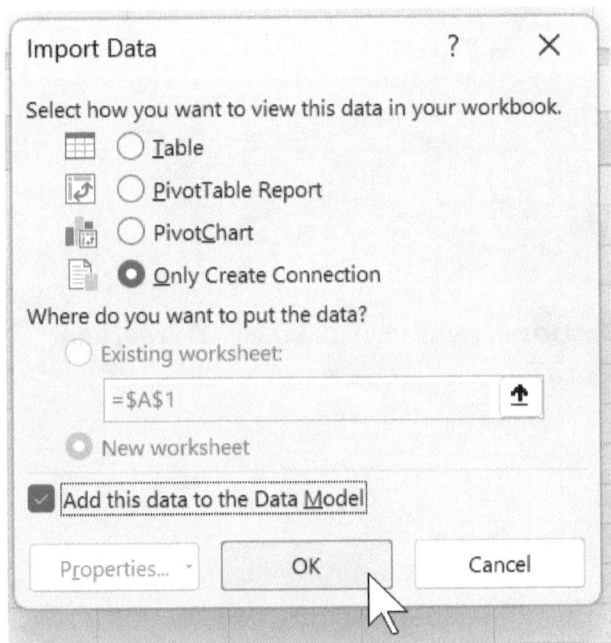

10. Excel will create **four** configurable queries that can be accessed by going to the **Data** tab and clicking on **Queries & Connections**.

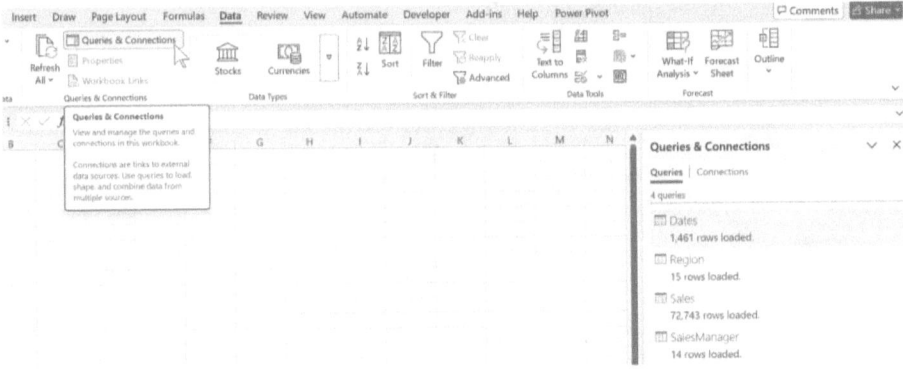

www.createandlearn.net

11. Go to the **File** tab and click on **Save As**. Save the file as **Sales Dashboard – Create and Learn**. Then, click **Save**.

12. Go to **Queries & Connections**, right-click the query **Dates**, and click on **Edit**.

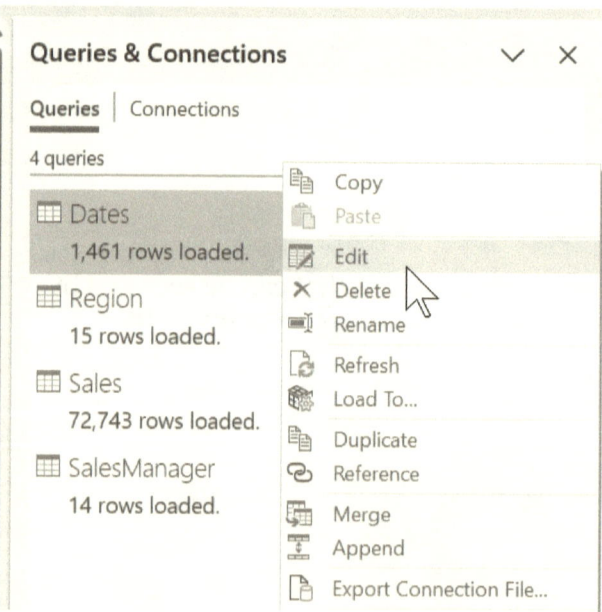

Get Data

13. The **Power Query Editor** window will open. This editor displays the data in the query and allows transformations in a friendly environment.

14. To create a new Columnn showing only the year, select the Columnn **FullDate** by clicking once on the Columnn title. Then, go to the **Add Columnn** tab, **Date**, option **Year**, and select **Year**.

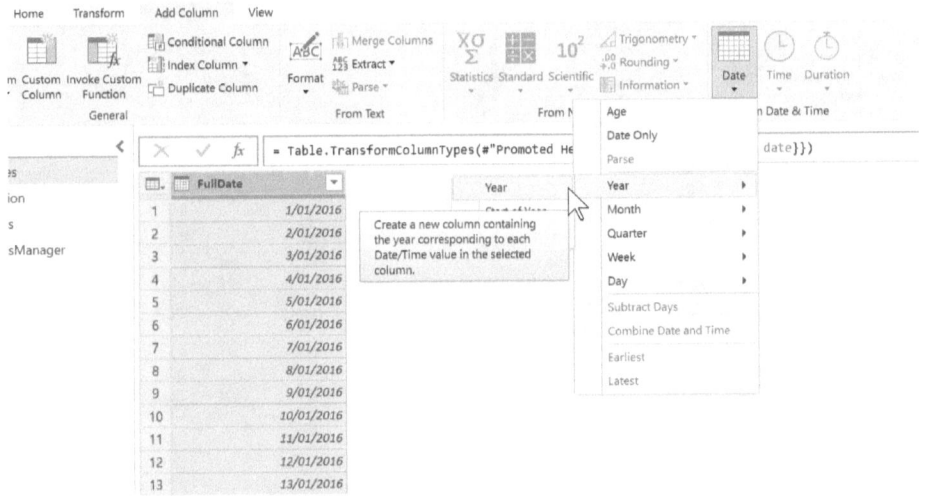

15. To create a Columnn showing the date as the start of the month, select the Columnn **FullDate**, go to the **Add Columnn** tab, **Date**, **Month**, and choose **Start of Month**.

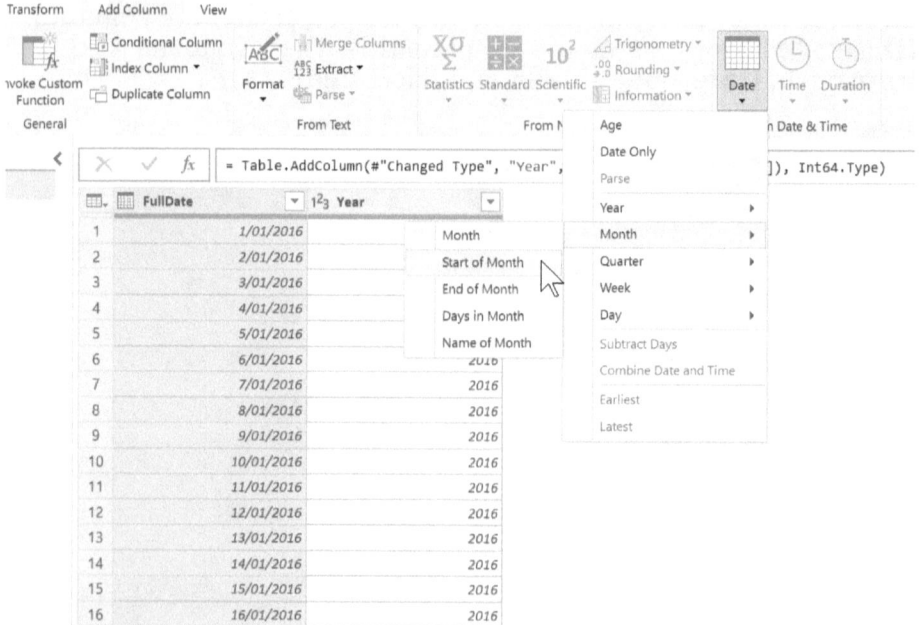

16. Go to the **Add Columnn** tab and click on **Custom Column**.

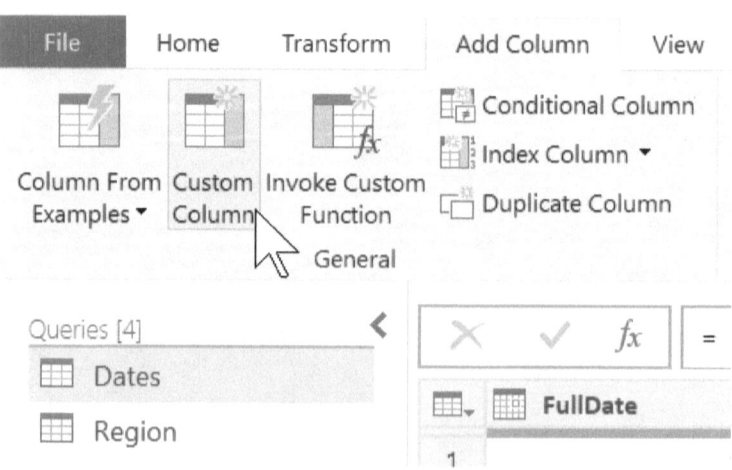

Get Data

17

17. In the **New Columnn name**, type **FY**. This custom Columnn will read the **FullDate** Columnn and show the financial year starting on July 1st of each year.

18. In the **Custom Columnn formula** area, type the formula (case sensitive):

= if Date.Month([FullDate])>6

then Date.Year([FullDate])+1

else Date.Year([FullDate])

Then, click **OK**.

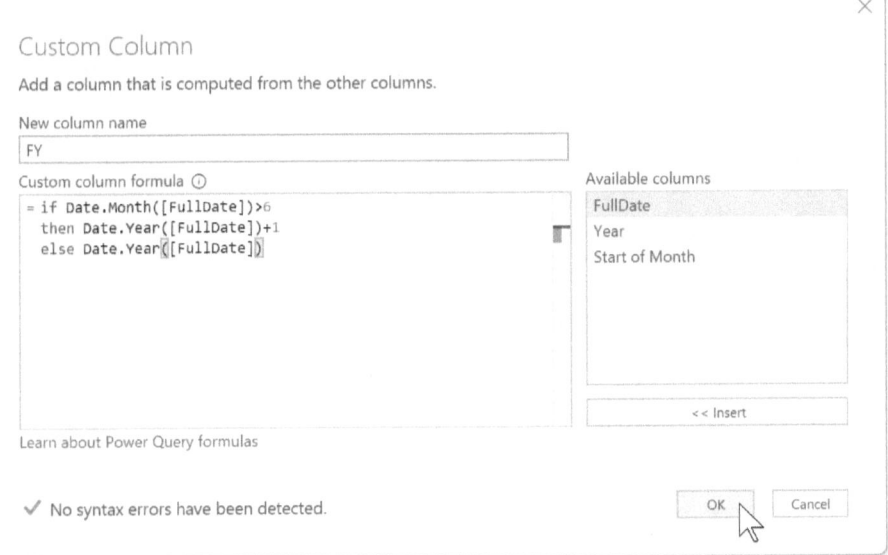

See the explanation:

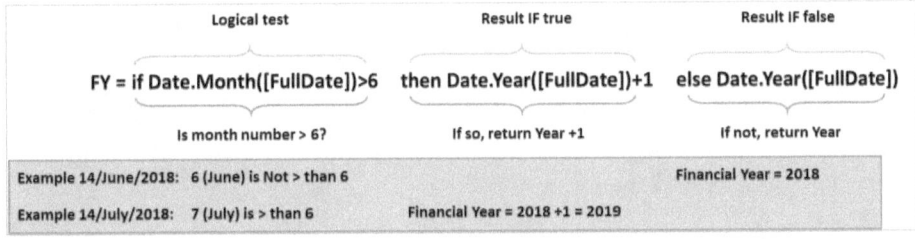

www.createandlearn.net

19. Note that Excel will create a step to be applied for each customization in the query. If needed, each step can be renamed, deleted, or moved.

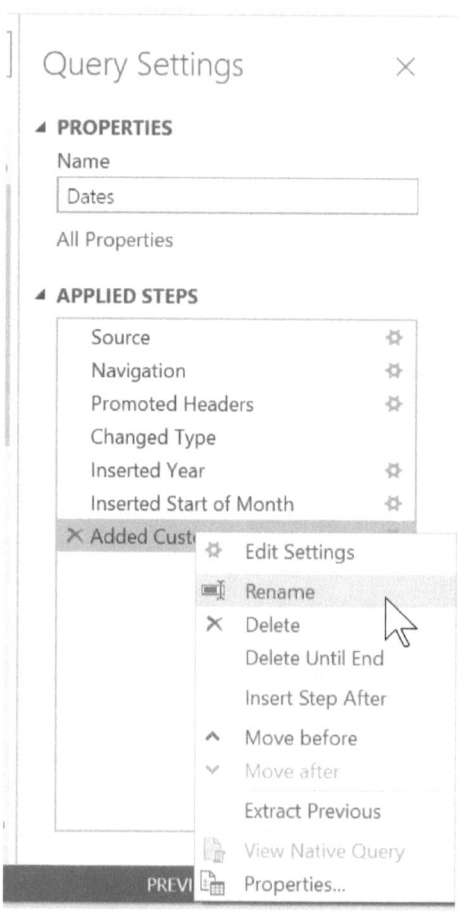

Get Data

20. Go to the **Home** tab and click on **Close & Load**.

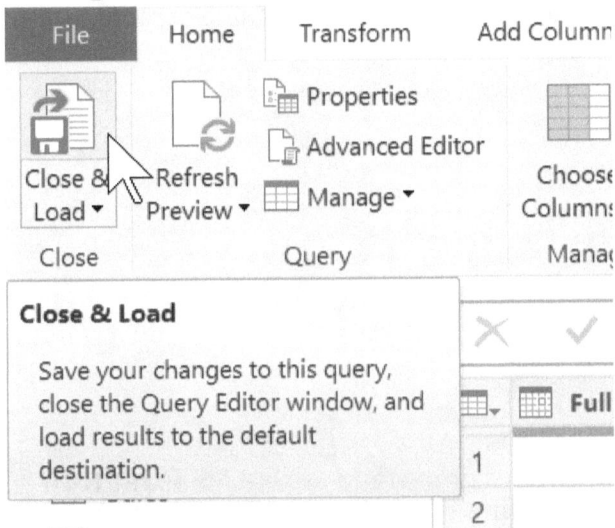

21. Go to **Queries & Connections**, right-click the query **Region**, and click on **Edit**.

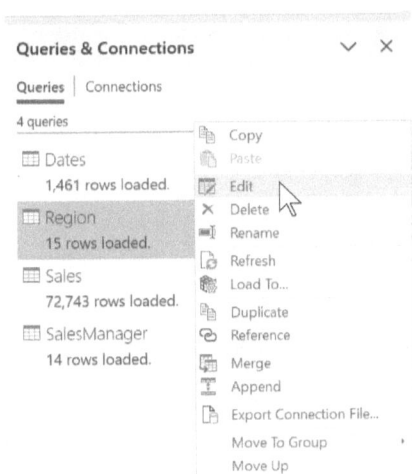

22. With the Power Query Editor opened, it is possible to see that the Columnns did **not** assume the correct title. It can happen with text fields where Excel cannot differentiate a title from standard table content.

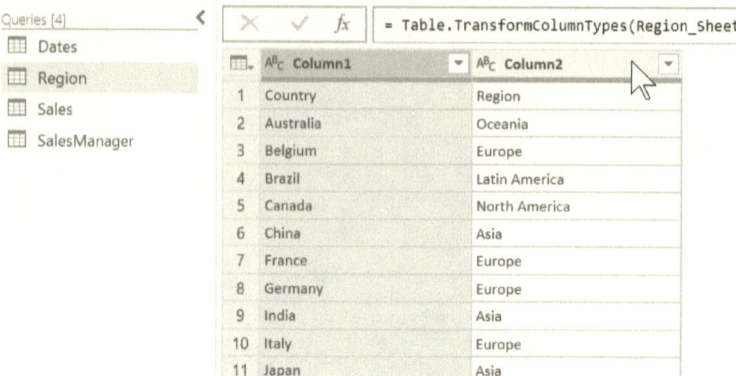

23 Go to the **Home** tab, **Transform** group, and select **Use First Row as Headers**. You will see that the first row is now the title of each Columnn.

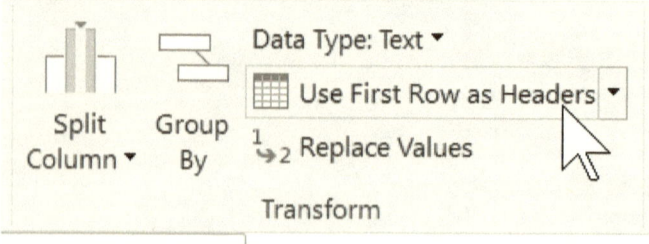

Get Data

24. Select the **Region** Columnn. Then, go to the **Transform** tab, click **Format**, and select **Capitalize Each Word**. This will give a proper capital letter to each word in the **Region** Columnn.

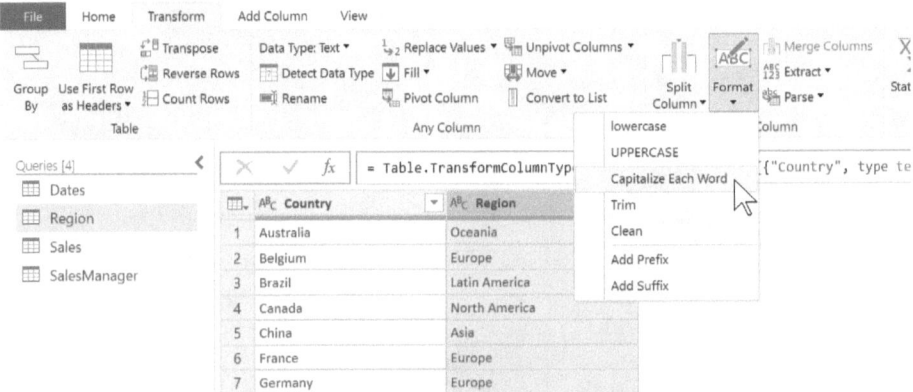

25. Go to the **Home** tab and click on **Close & Load**.

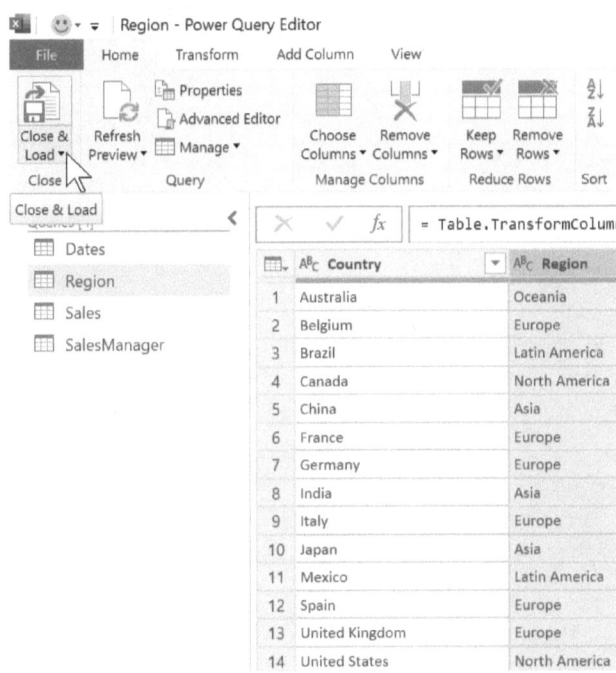

www.createandlearn.net

26. Go to the **Queries** pane and select **Sales**.

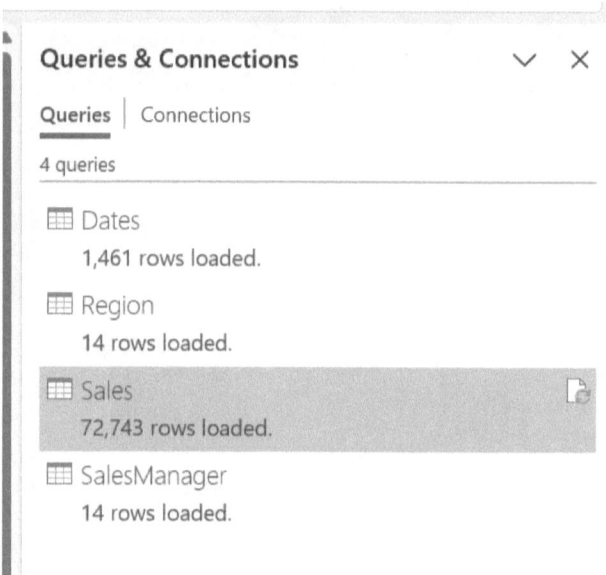

Get Data

27. Go to the **Add Columnn** tab and click on **Custom Column**.

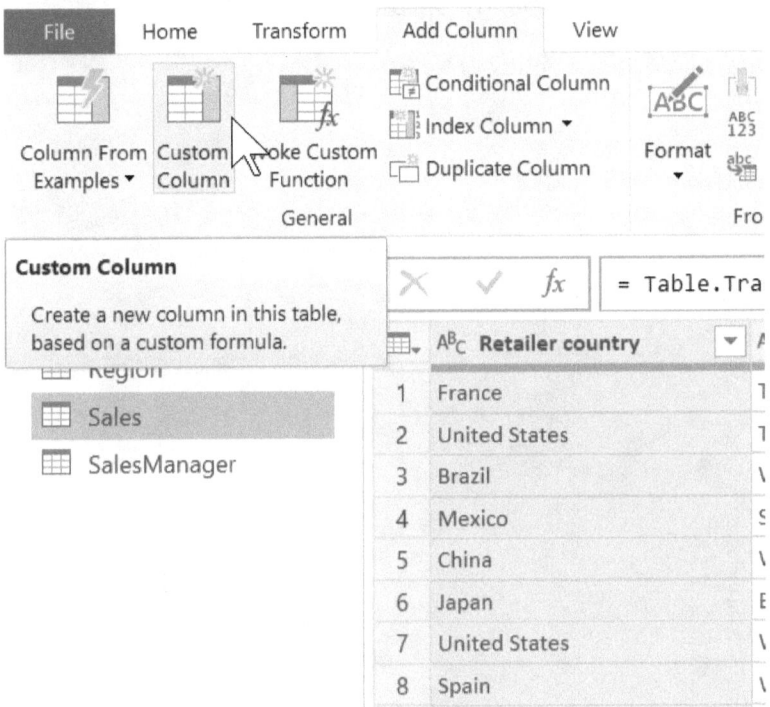

28. In the **New Columnn name** field, type **Total Cost**. Then, in the **Custom Columnn formula** type, the formula:

=[Unit Cost]*[Quantity] .Then, click **OK**.

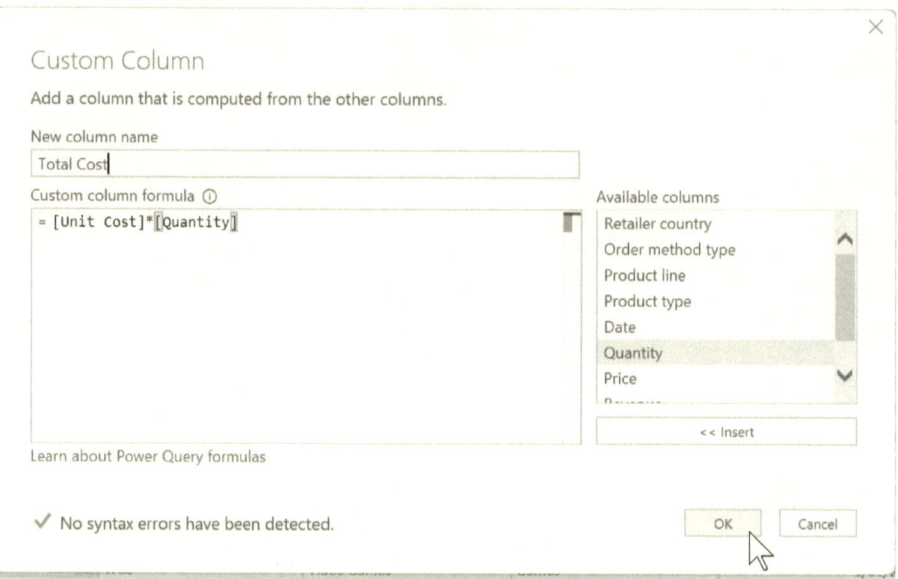

See the explanation:

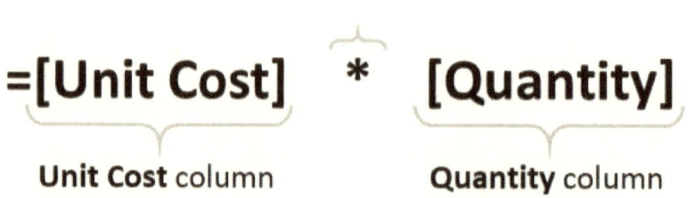

Get Data

25

29. Go to the **Add Columnn** tab and click on **Custom Column**.

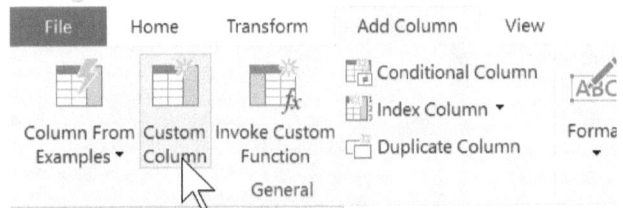

30. In the **New Columnn** name field, type **Gross Result**. Then, in the Custom Columnn formula type, the formula =[Revenue]-[Total Cost] . Then, click **OK**.

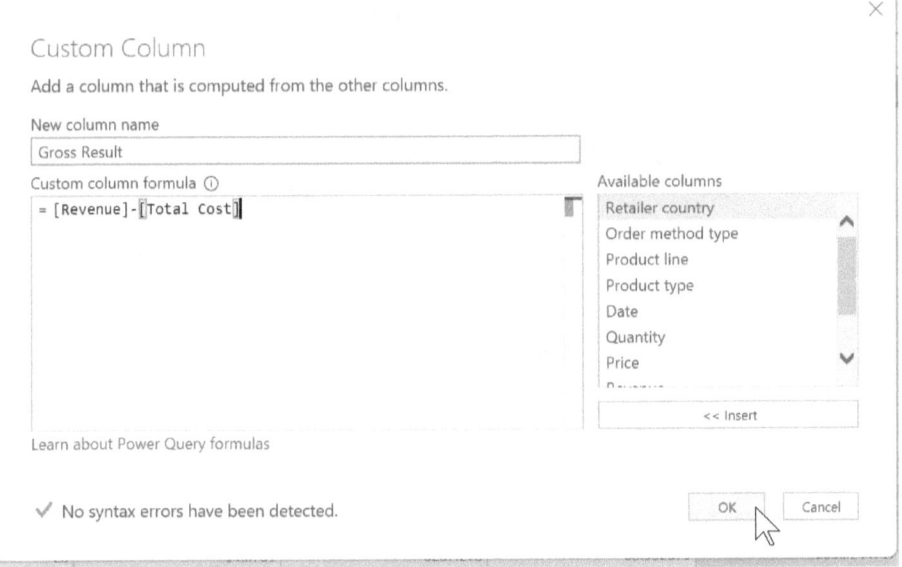

See the explanation:

31. Note that the new Columnns applied their formula in each row.

www.createandlearn.net

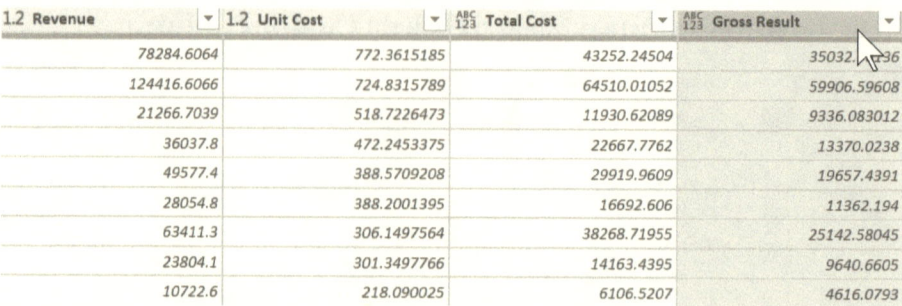

32. Select the Columnns **Price** to **Gross Result** (Click on Price, hold the **Shift** key, and click on Gross Result). Then, go to the **Home** tab, **Data Type**, and click on **Currency**. It will **add a new step**.

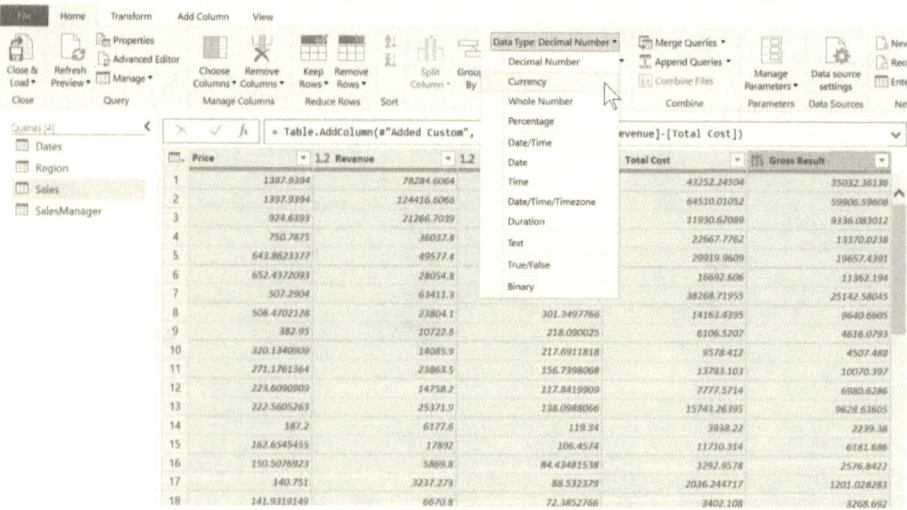

Get Data

33. Note that new steps were applied.

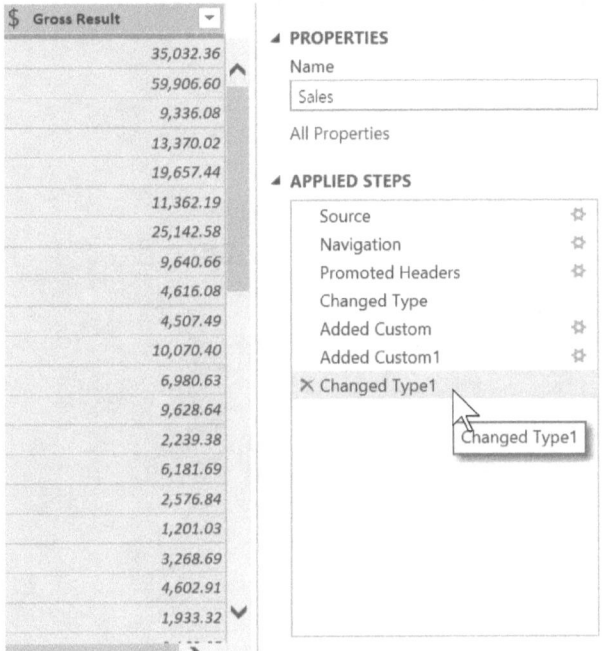

34. Go to the **Queries** pane and select **SalesManager**.

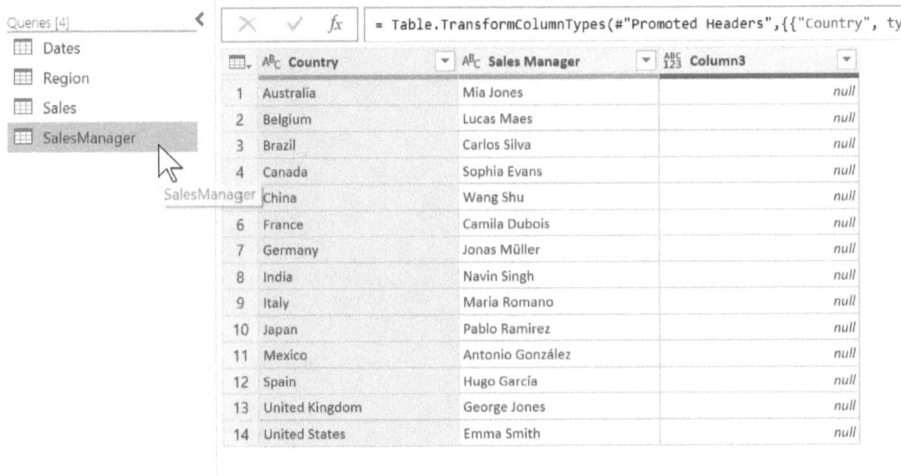

35. This table has an unwanted Columnn. Select **Columnn 3**, go to the **Home** tab, and click **Remove Columnns**.

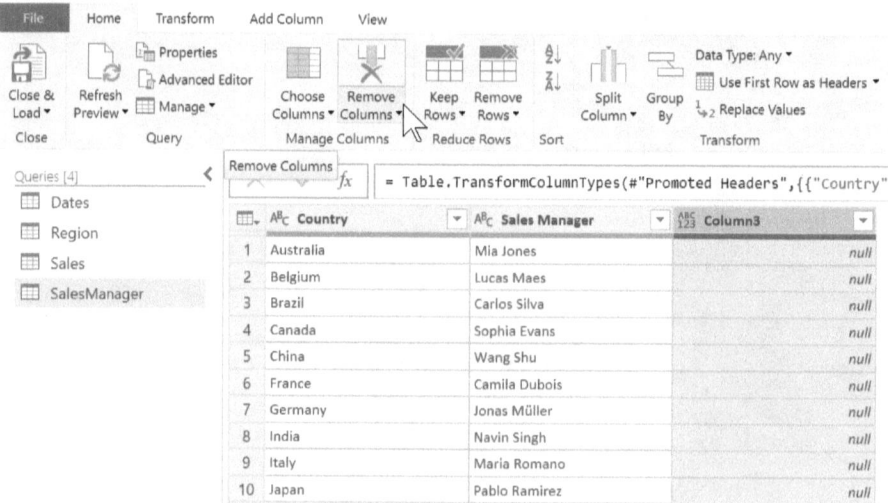

Get Data

36. Go to the **Home** tab and click on **Close & Load**.

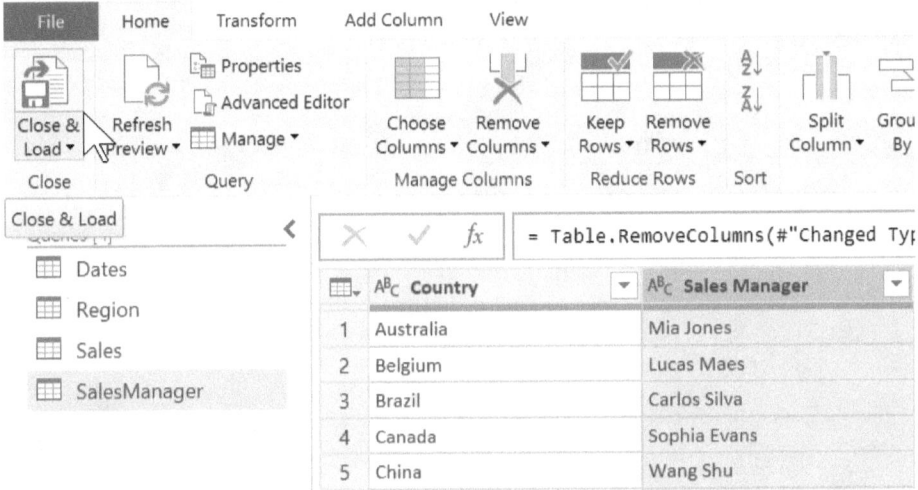

37. Double-click the tab **Sheet1** and change the name to **Sales Dashboard**. Then, click on **New sheet** and give the name **PivotTables**.

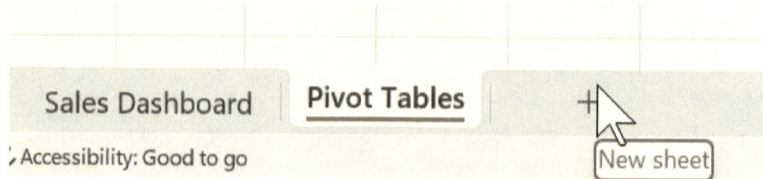

Get Data

38. Go to the **Sales Dashboard** tab.

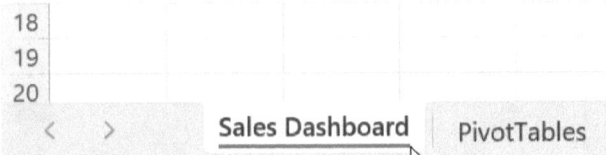

39. Click **Save a Copy**.

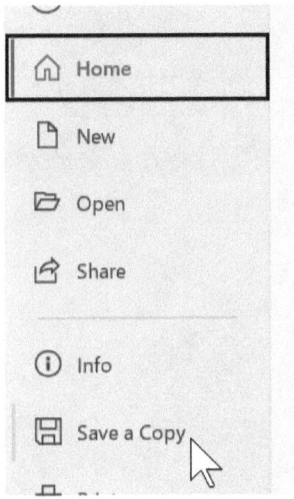

40. Go to the **Page Layout** tab, **Gridlines**, and deselect the **View** box. This action will clean the gridlines in the current tab.

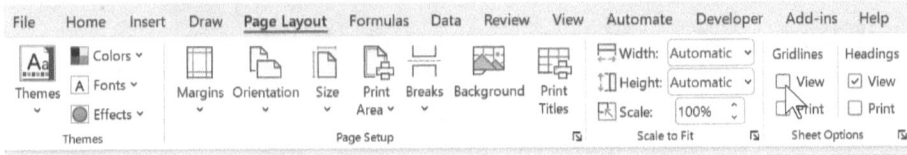

41. Select Cells from **A1** to **Q43** (A1:Q43).

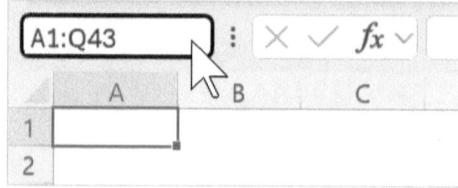

42. Go to the **Home** tab and change the **Fill Color** to **Light Gray**.

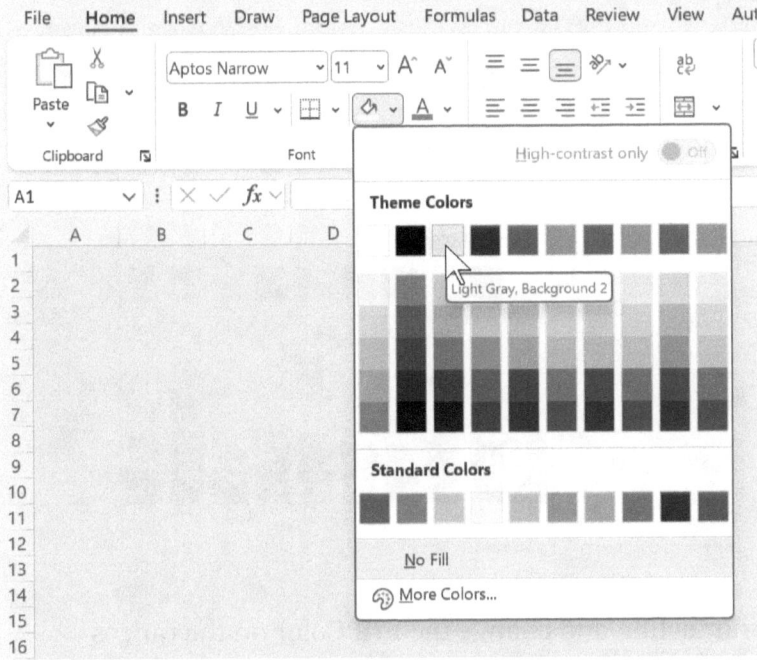

43. Select cells **B2:D3**. Then, change the **Fill Color** to **White**.

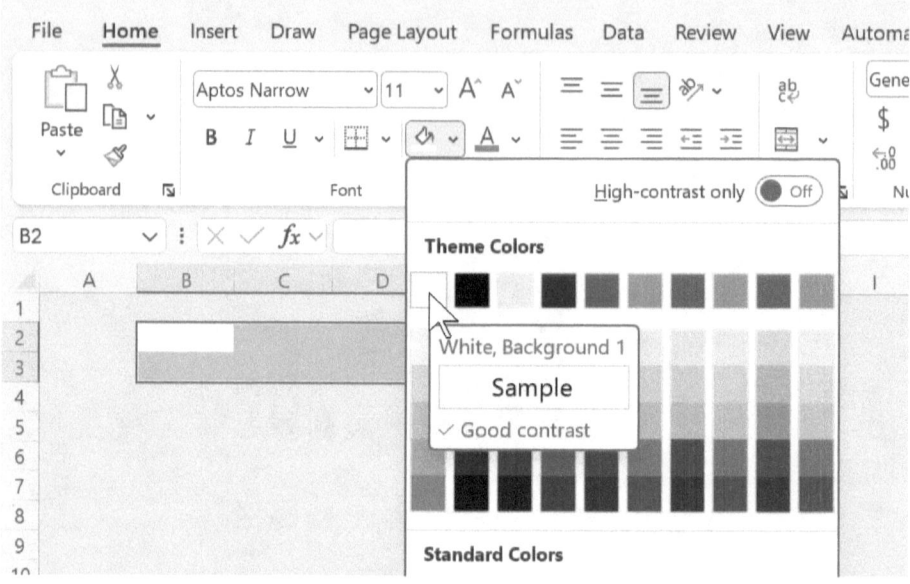

44. Repeat the prior action and change the **Fill** Color on the ranges **F2:F3**, **H2:H3**, and **J2:J3**.

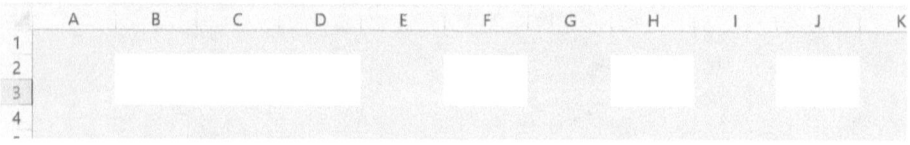

45. Hold the **Ctrl** key and select Columnns **A**, **E**, **G**, and **I**.

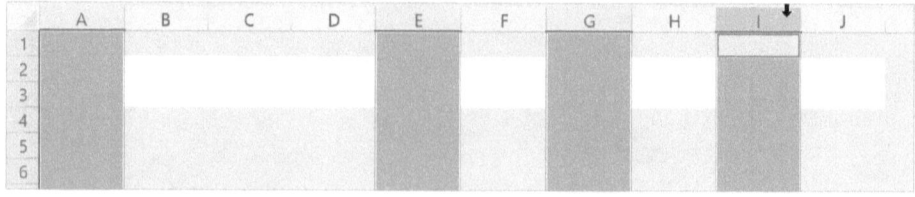

Get Data

46. Right-click any selection and select **Columnn** Width. Change the **width** to 0.94 (17 pixels).

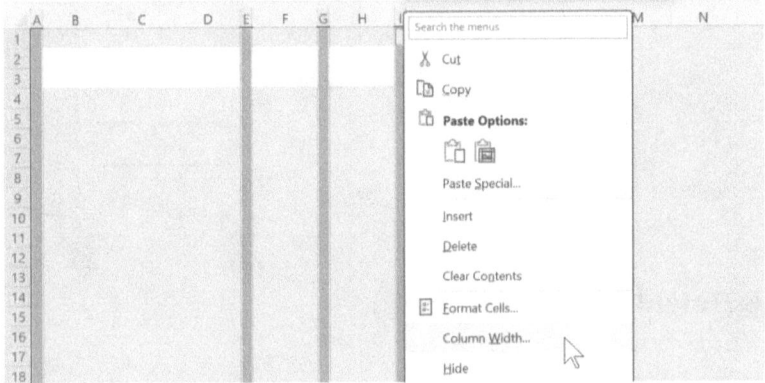

47. Hold the **Ctrl** key and select Columnns **F**, **H**, and **J**.

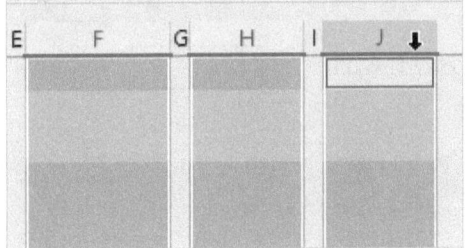

48. Change the Columnn **Width** to 34.00 (381 pixels).

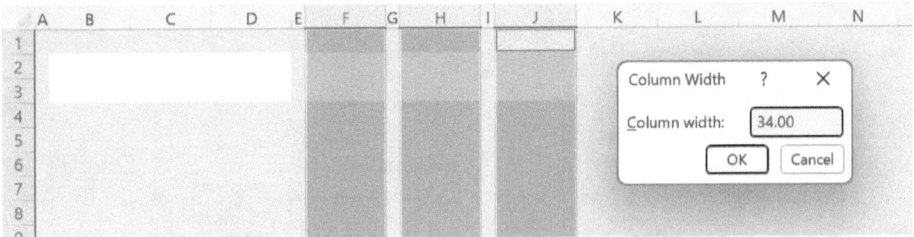

49. Select row 2. Then, right-click it and select **Row Height**. Change row **Height** to 73.50 (147 pixels).

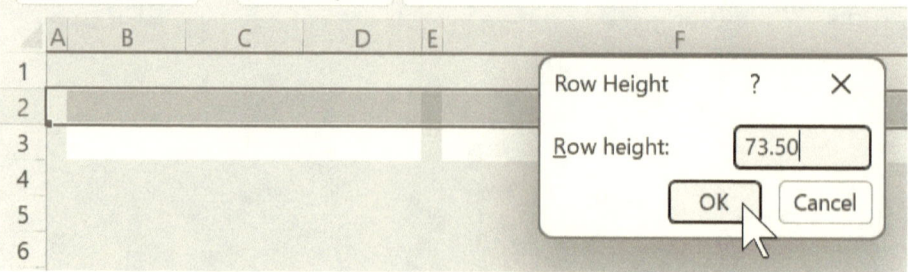

50. Change row 3 **Height** to 40.50 (81 pixels).

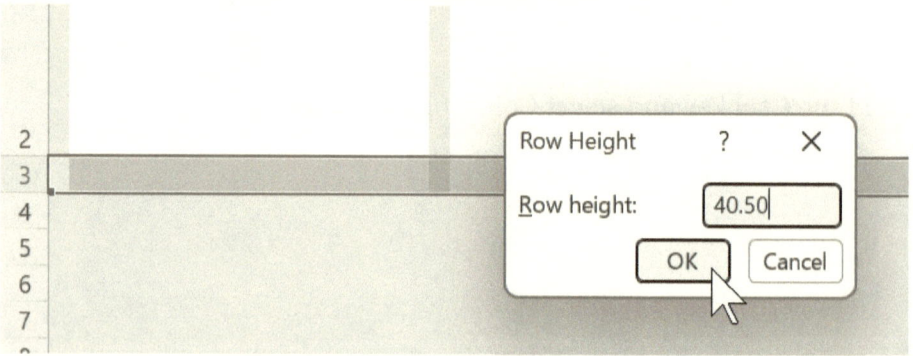

51. Select Columnns **B**, **C**, and **D** and change their **width** to 16.43 (188 pixels).

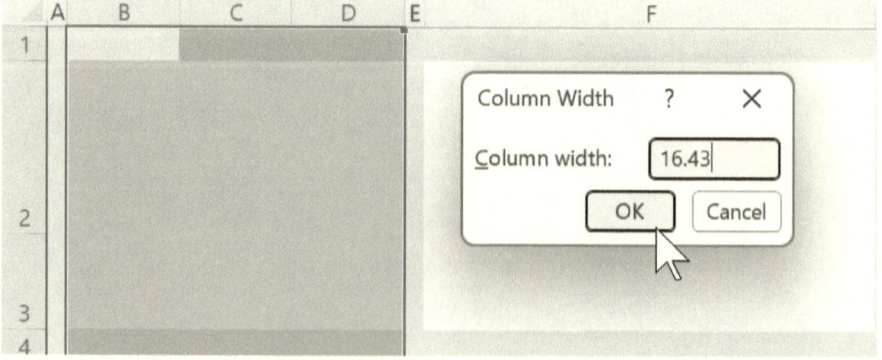

52. Select Columnn **K:Q** (K to Q) and change their **width** to 11.73 (136 pixels).

Get Data

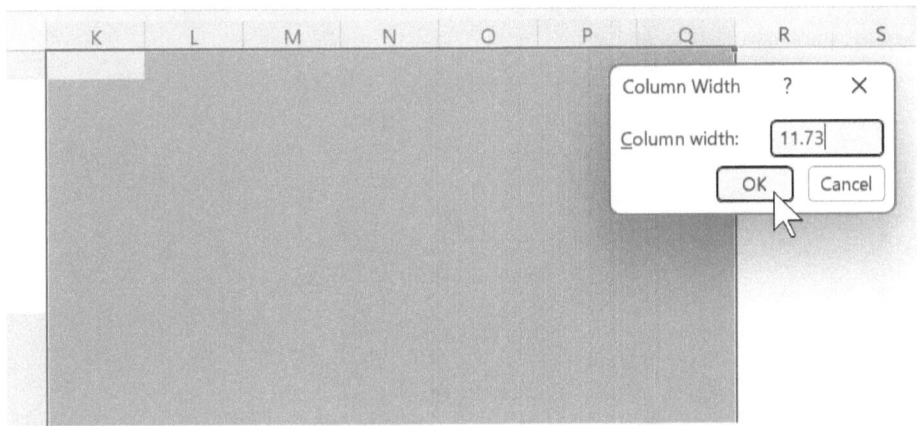

53. Visit the web address **createandlearn.net/bifiles** and save the Create and Learn image by right-clicking and selecting **Save image as**. If it asks for a **password**, type **bifiles**

54. Go to the **Insert** tab, **Pictures, Place over Cells,** and click on **This Device**.

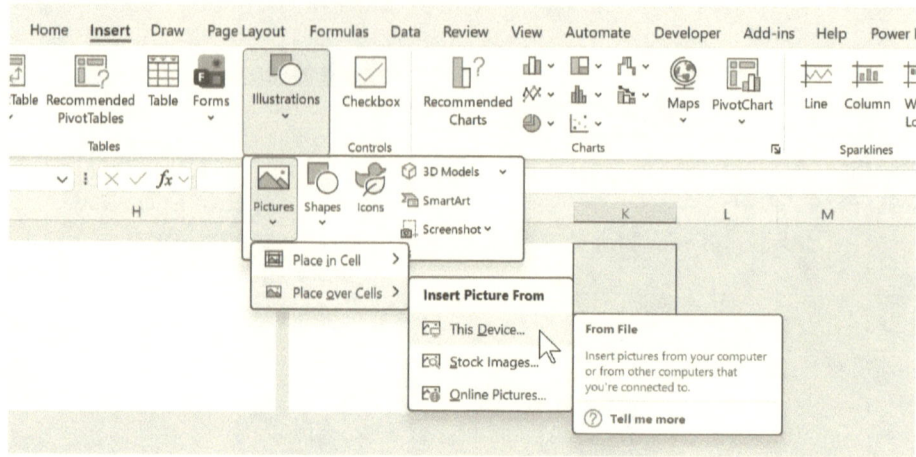

55. Select the downloaded image **Logo.png** and click on **Insert**.

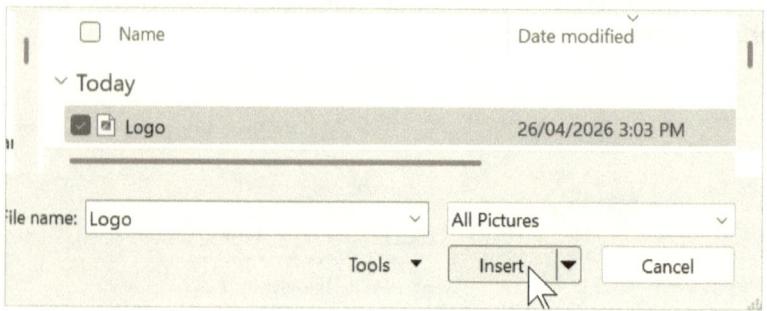

56. Select the image and go to the **Picture Format** tab, **Size**, and change the height to **2.59 cm (1.02")** and width to **9.43 cm (3.63")**.

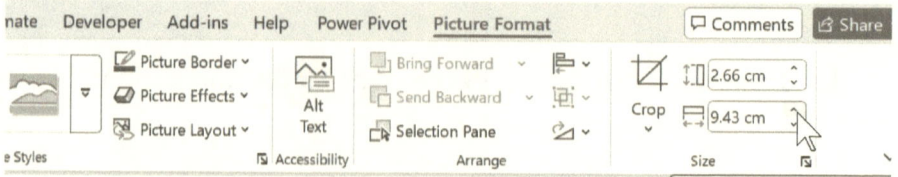

57. Drag and drop the image to the middle of Columnns **B:D**.

Get Data

58. In cells F3, H3, and J3, type the titles **Revenue**, **Total Cost**, and **Gross Margin** as shown in the image below.

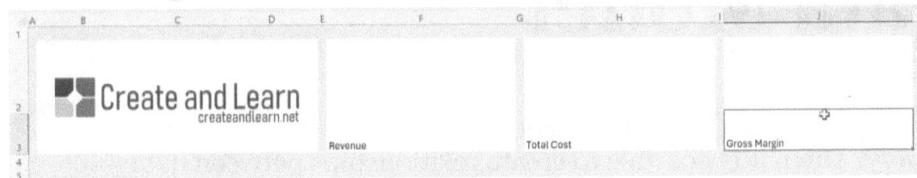

59. Select range F3:J3. Then, go to the **Home** tab and change the **Font size** to 16, set alignment to **Center** and **Middle,** and **Font Color** to White, Darker 50%.

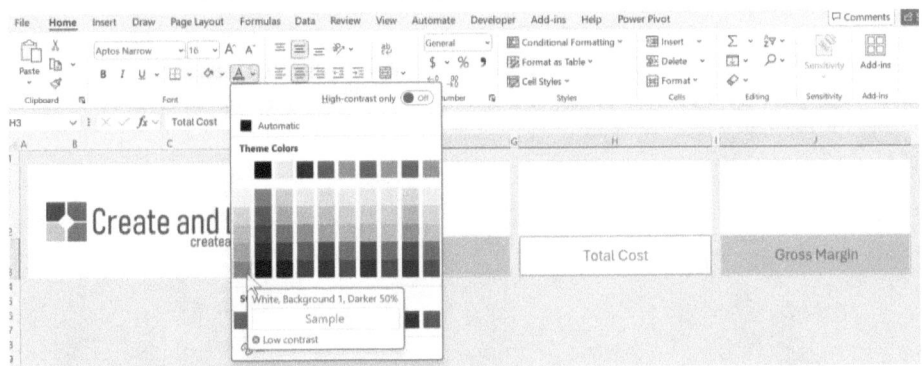

www.createandlearn.net

Chapter 3
Data Model

The data model is a powerful Excel tool that loads the data in Excel's memory. Then, it is possible to create relationships between data without using formulas such as INDEX, MATCH, or VLOOKUP. The data can then be used to create reports and visuals through PivotTable (Power Pivot) and Power Charts.

Also, you can use the DAX (Data Analysis Expressions) formula to create new information from the data you already have in your Data Model.

1. Go to the **Power Pivot** Data Model tab and click **Manage**.

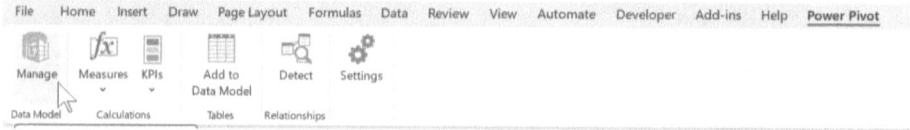

Data Model

2. In the **Data Model** window, go to the **Home** tab and click on **Diagram View**.

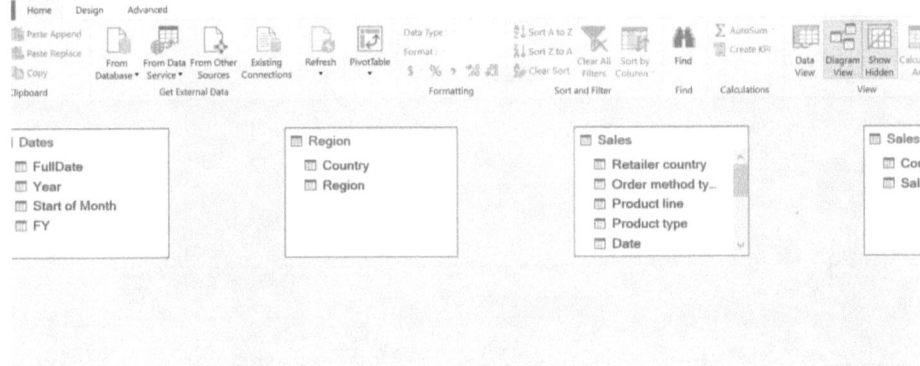

3. The imported tables will be displayed.

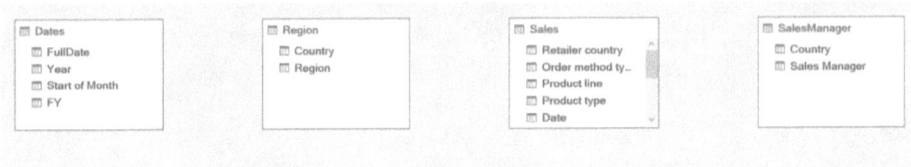

4. Drag and drop the tables to organize them, as shown in the image below. You can resize them as well.

Sales
- Retailer country
- Order method type
- Product line
- Product type
- Date
- Quantity
- Price
- Revenue
- Unit Cost
- Total Cost
- Gross Result

Dates
- FullDate
- Year
- Start of Month
- FY

Region
- Country
- Region

SalesManager
- Country
- Sales Manager

Data Model

5. To create a relationship, link the fields. As in the image below, click on the **FullDate** field and drag it to connect with the **Date** field in the **Sales** table.

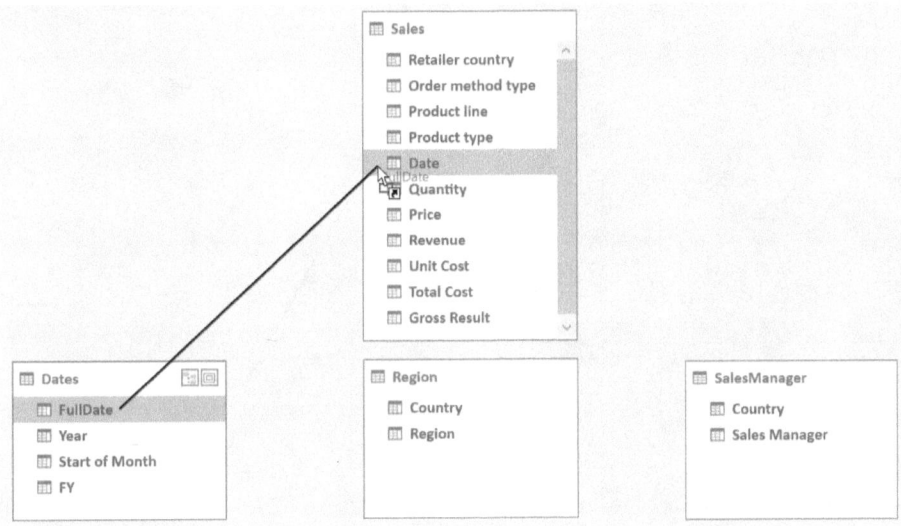

6. Create a relationship between the **Retailer country** and the **Country** in the **Region** table.

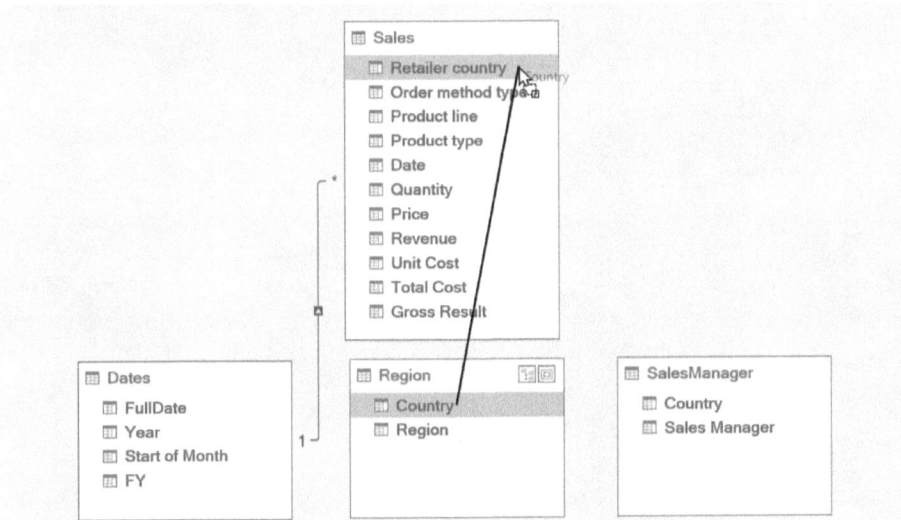

7. Create a link between **Retailer country** and **Country** in the **SalesManager** table.

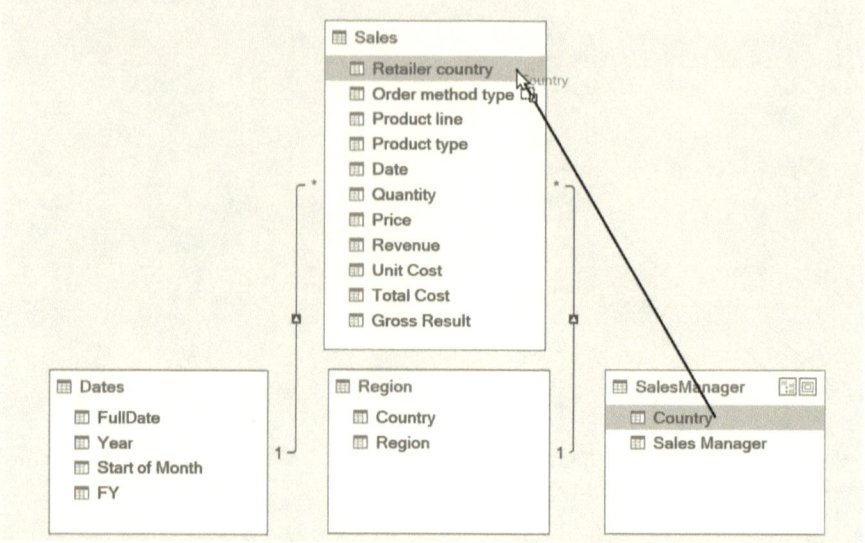

8. If you roll the mouse over the lines, the related fields will be highlighted.

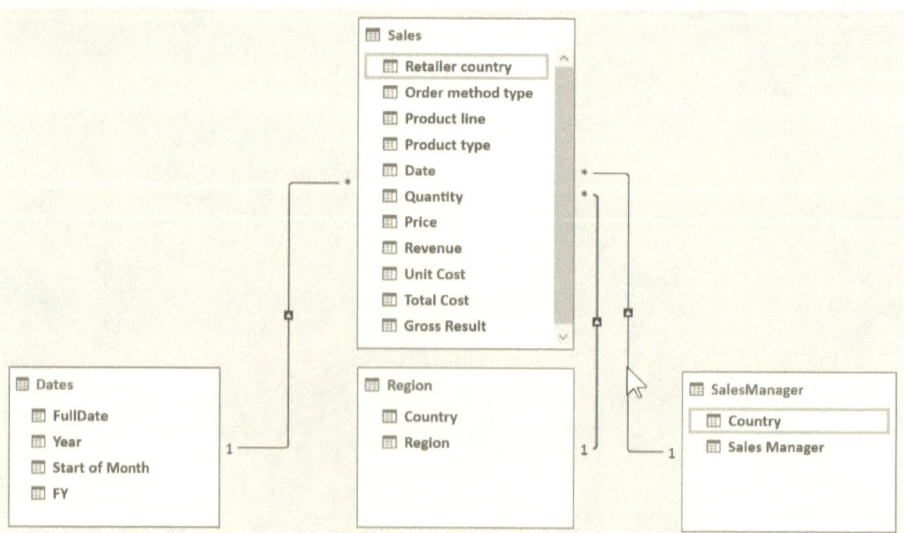

9. To edit the relationship, double-click the connector line. Click **Cancel**.

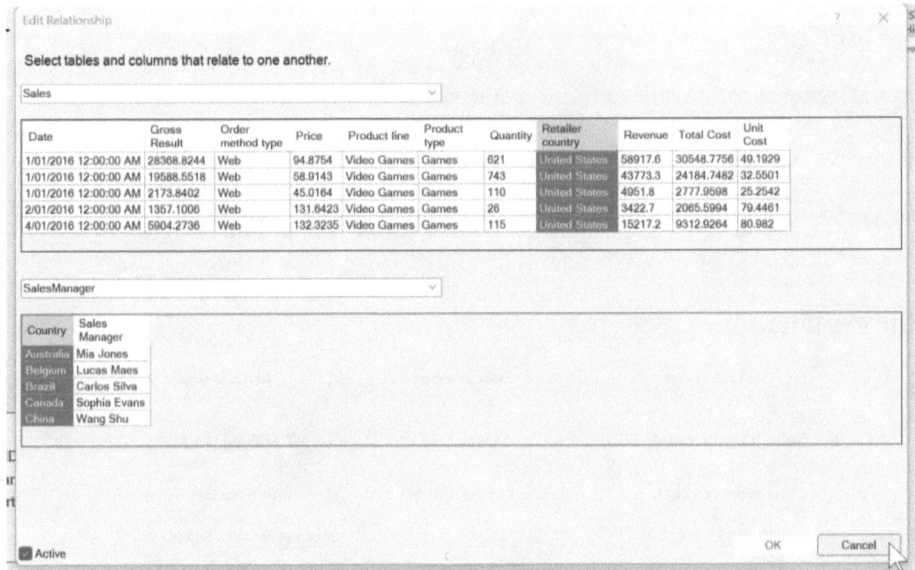

10. Go to the Home tab and click on **Data View**.

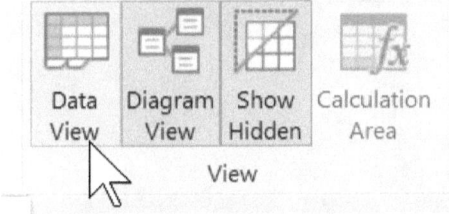

11. Select the **Sales** tab.

12. Click on the first row of the **Add Columnn** and type the formula:
=if(Sales[Quantity]>500,"Over 500","500 or Under")

Press Enter

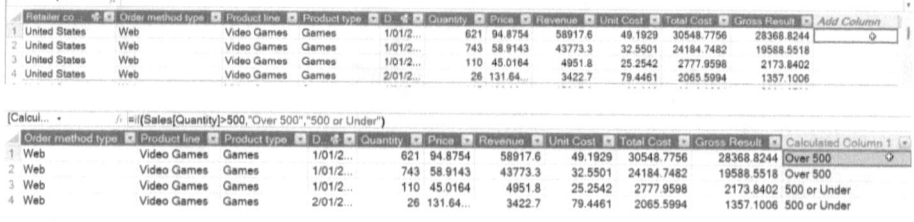

See the explanation:

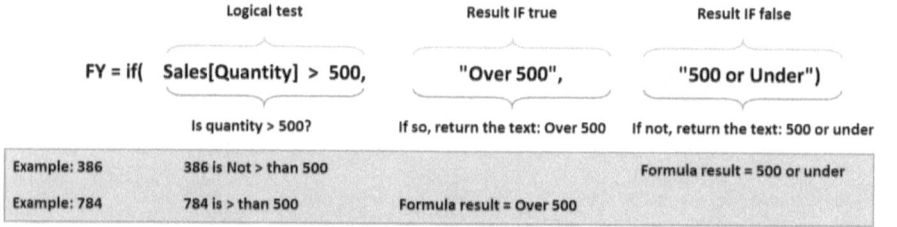

13. Double-click the new **Calculated Columnn 1** title and change it to **IF Study**.

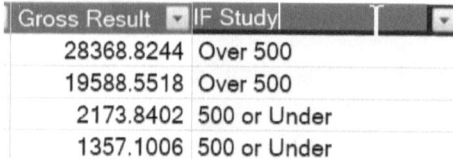

14. Go to the next Add Columnn.

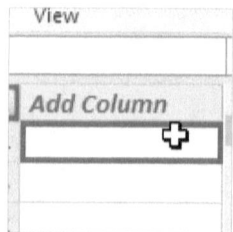

Data Model

47

15. Click on the first row of the **Add Columnn** and type the formula:
=Sales[Price]*Sales[Quantity]

Press Enter

See explanation:

=Sales[Price] * Sales[Quantity]

Multiplication

Price column   **Quantity** column

16. Double-click the title and change the name to **Multiplication Study**.
17. Click on the first row of the next **Add Columnn** and type the formula:

=Sales[Retailer country]&" - "&Sales[Product line]

Press Enter

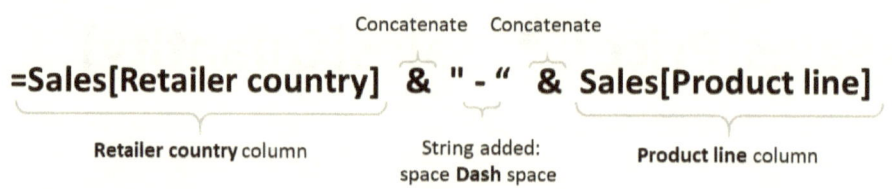

See explanation:

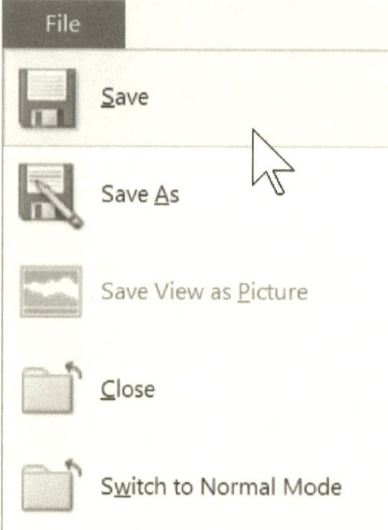

18. Change the Columnn name to **Concat Study**.
19. Go to the **File** tab and click on **Save.** Then, close the Power Pivot window.

Data Model

5. Measures

Excel Measures, also known as calculated fields, are a critical tool in Power Pivot. They are frequently utilized during data analysis and provide a way to calculate results in relation to relevant factors, such as total sales based on time, location, organization, or product.

1. Go to the **Power Pivot** tab, **Measures**, and click on **New Measure**.

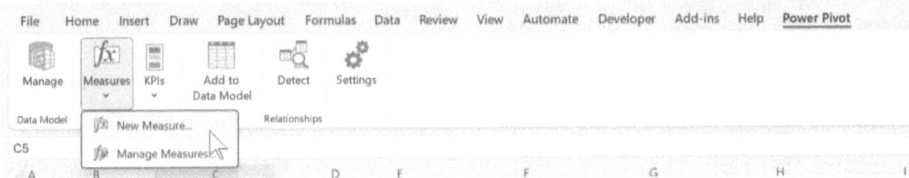

2. In the **Measure** window, select **Sales** as Table name, type **Gross Margin** as the Measure name, select Category **Number**, Format **Percentage,** Decimal places **0**, and type the formula:

=(sum(Sales[Revenue])- sum(Sales[Total Cost])) / sum(Sales[Revenue])

Then click **OK**.

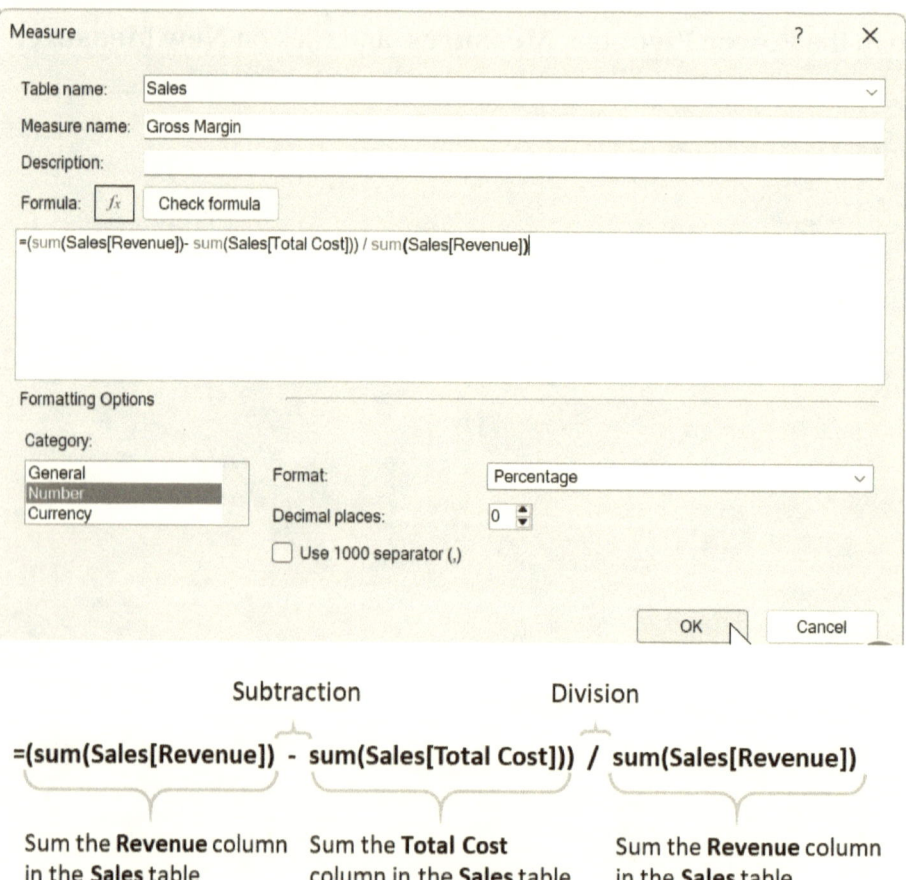

Chapter 4
Creating (Power) PivotCharts

Power PivotCharts describes a standard **PivotChart** that can access the whole data model, allowing the user to create a PivotChart using data from the **Data Model** tool, containing multiple sources and custom calculations.

6. Clustered Columnn

1. Go to the **Insert** tab, **Charts**, and click on **PivotChart**.

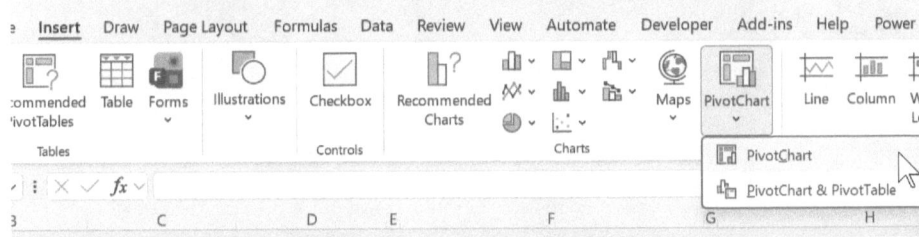

2. In the **Create PivotChart** window, check the item **Use this workbook's Data Model** and **Existing Worksheet**. Then set the **Location** as 'Sales Dashboard'!$B$5 and click **OK**.

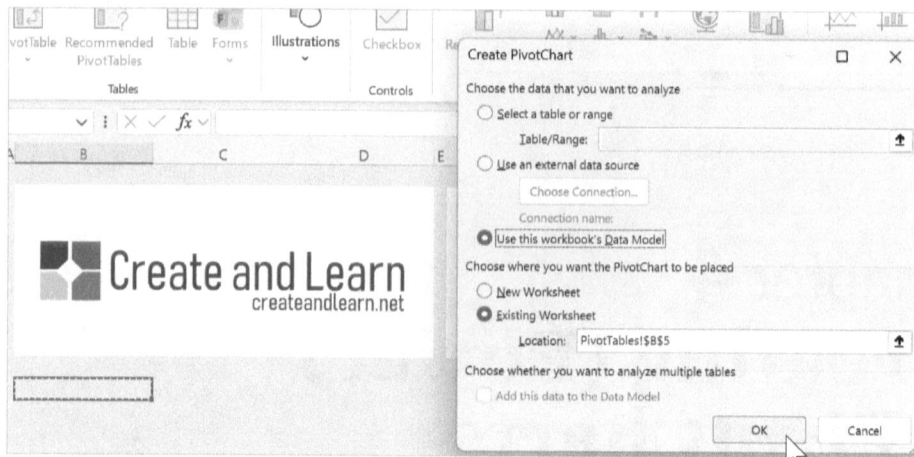

Note: To easily select cell B5, click on the **arrow button**. Then, select the cell B5 and press **Enter**.

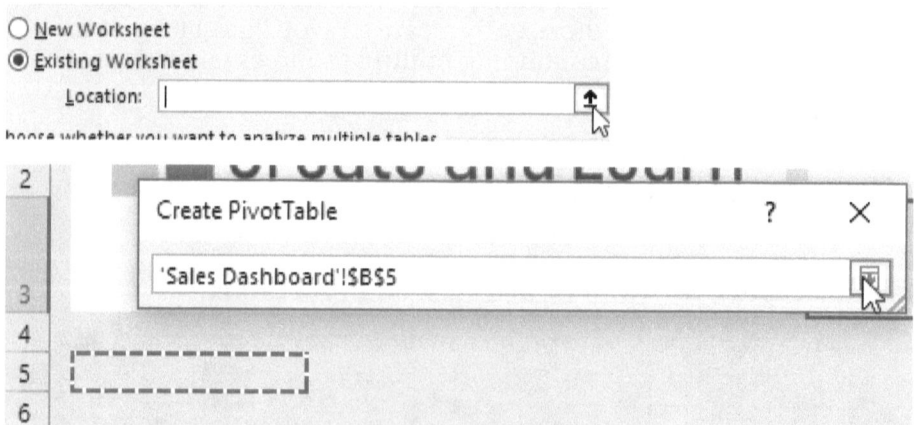

Creating (Power) PivotCharts

3. A blank PivotTable will be created, and all the tables and fields from the imported file will be available in the **PivotTable Fields** section. Click the arrow to collapse or expand the fields, as shown in the image below.

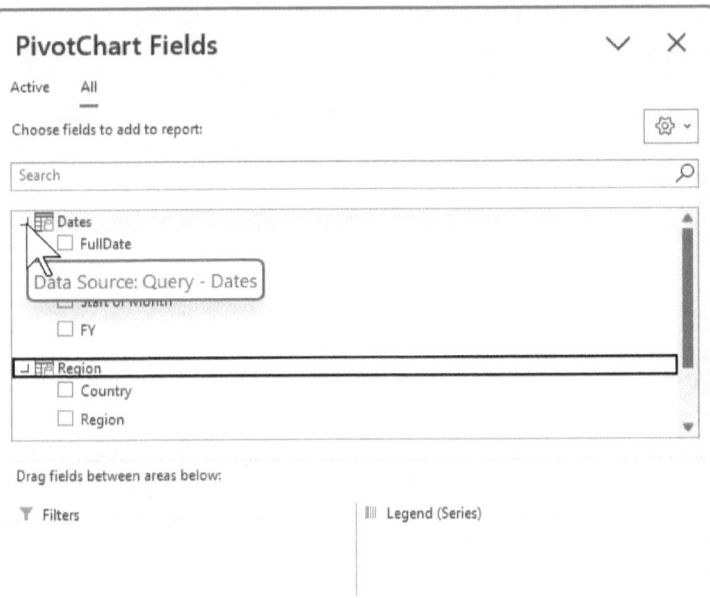

4. Add the field **Year** in the **Axis (Categories)** section and the field **Revenue** in the **Value** section. The fields can be moved by dragging, dropping, or right-clicking and selecting the area.

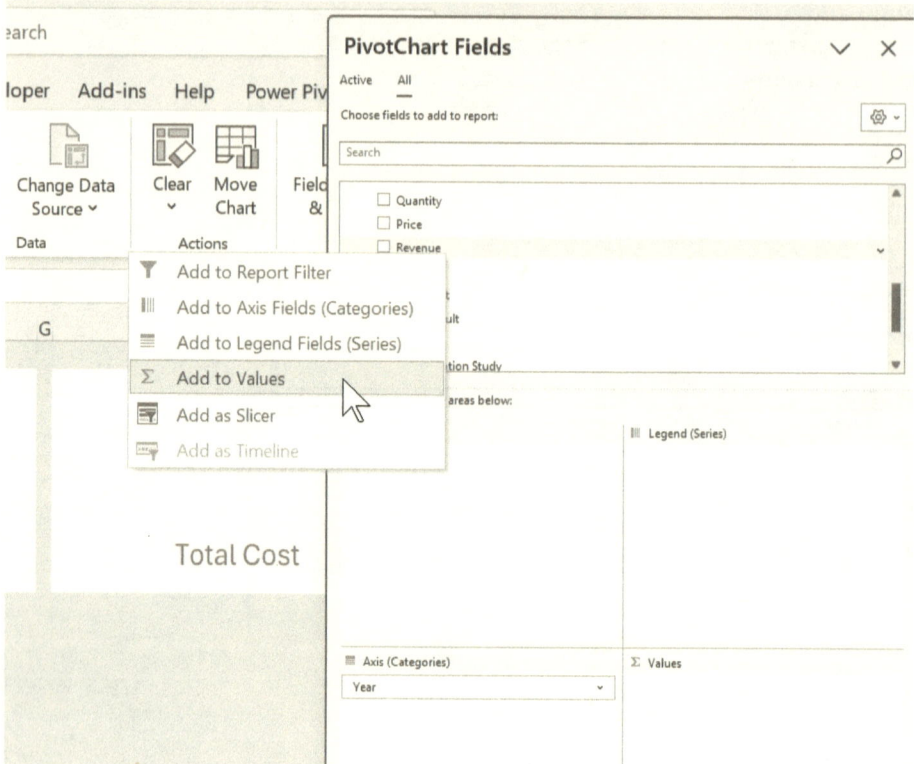

Creating (Power) PivotCharts

5. Select the PivotChart

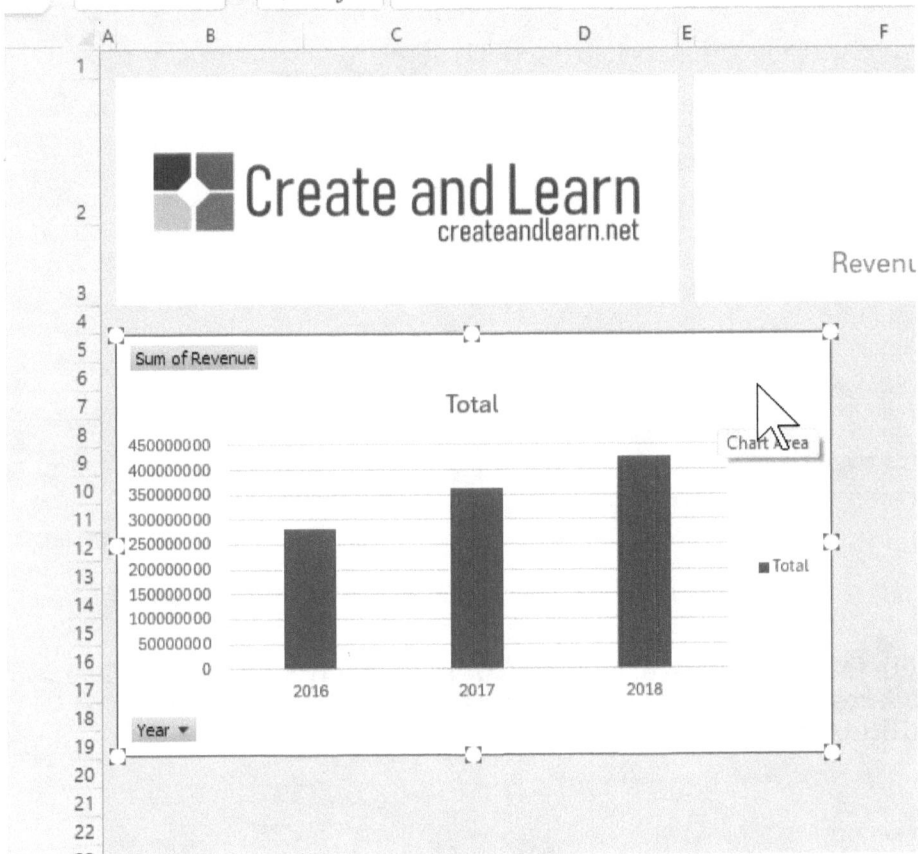

6. Go to the **PivotChart Analyze** tab, click on **Field Buttons**, and select **Hide All**.

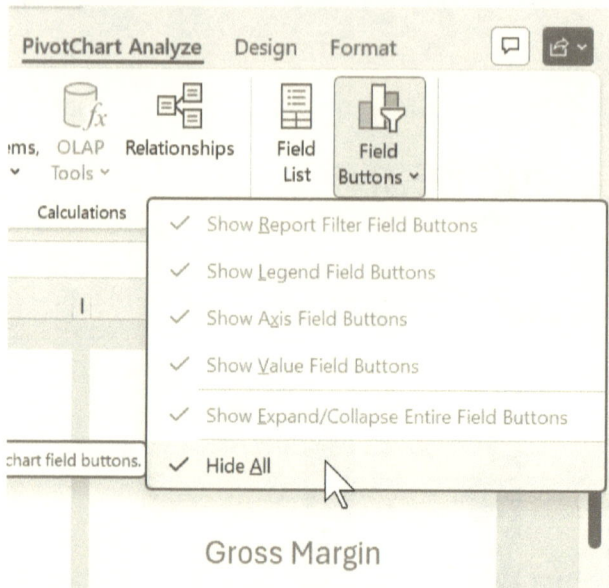

7. With the chart selected, click on **Chart Elements** ("+" icon). Then, go to **Axes** and select only **Primary Horizontal**. Also, uncheck **Gridlines** and **Legend**.

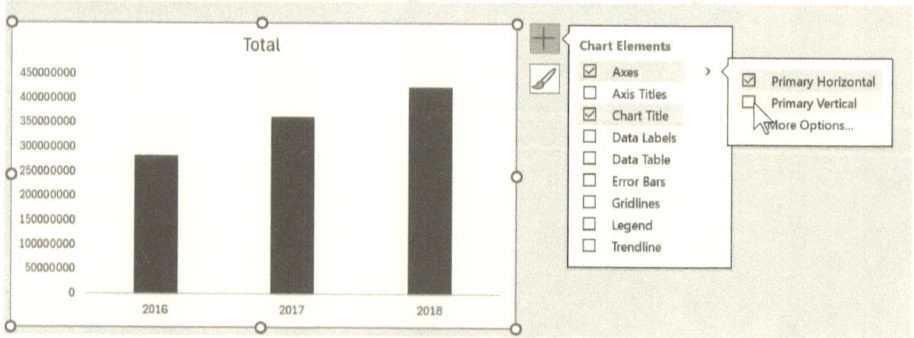

Creating (Power) PivotCharts

8. Right-click any bar and click on **Format Data Series**.

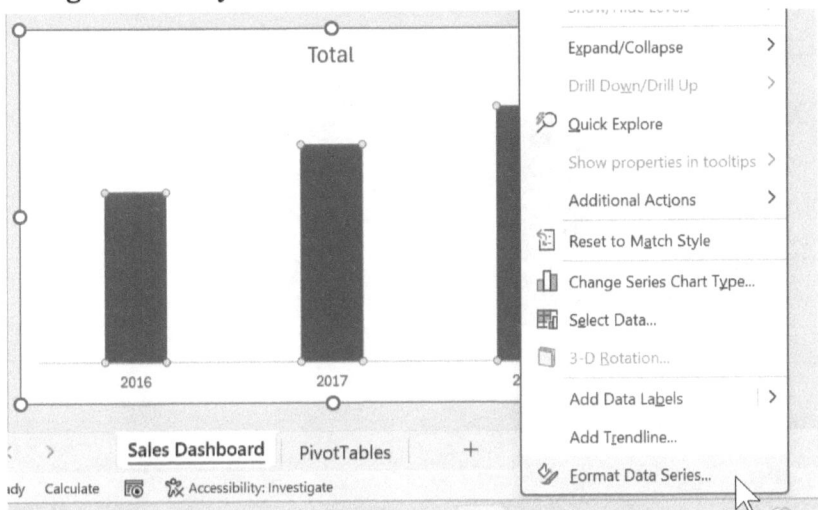

9. Go to **Series Options** and change **Series Overlap** to 0% and **Gap Width** to 100%.

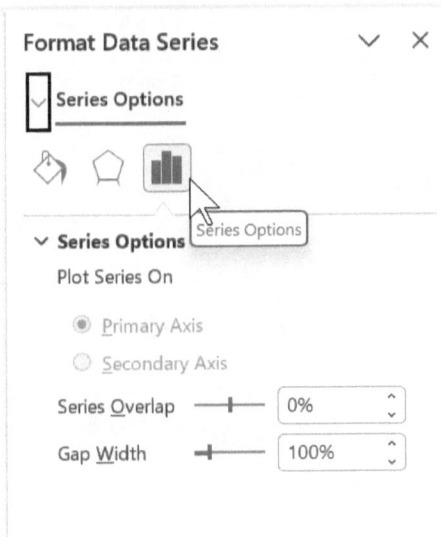

10. Go to **Chart Elements**, check **Data Labels**, and go to **More Options**.

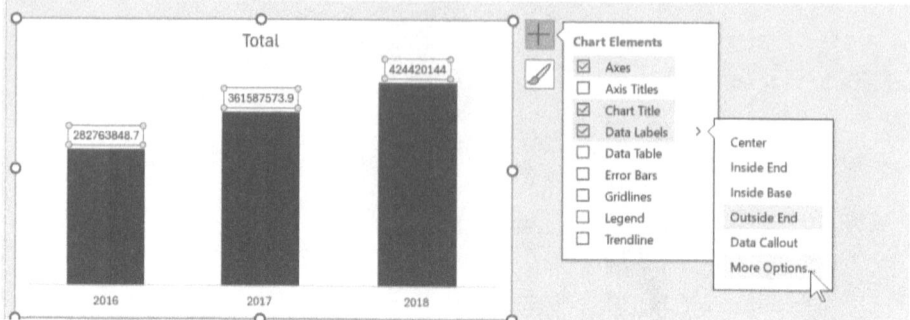

Creating (Power) PivotCharts 59

11. Go to **Label Options**, **Number**, and change **Category** to **Custom**. Then, type in the **Format Code** field the new format #,,"M". **Then** click Add. This will change how the number will be shown in the Data Labels.

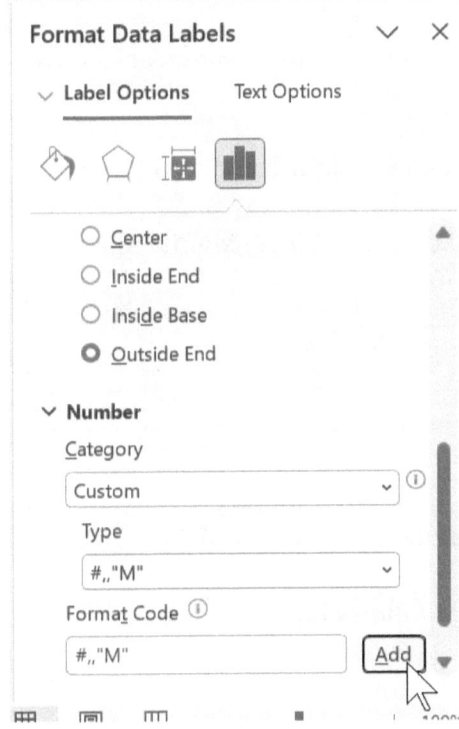

12. In the table below, I have included the most common custom format codes that can be used to change the way the data is shown:

Format Code	Description
#	Digit placeholder that represents optional digits and does not display extra zeros.
0	Digit placeholder that displays insignificant zeros.
?	Digit placeholder that leaves a space for insignificant zeros but doesn't display them.
@	Text placeholder
. (period)	Decimal point
, (comma)	Thousands separator. A comma that follows a digit placeholder scales the number by a thousand.
\	Displays the character that follows it.
" "	Display any text enclosed in double quotes.
%	Multiplies the numbers entered in a cell by 100 and displays the percentage sign.
/	Represents decimal numbers as fractions.
* (asterisk)	Repeats the character that follows it until the cell's width is filled. It's often used in combination with the space character to change alignment.

Creating (Power) PivotCharts

13. Click on any label to select them all.

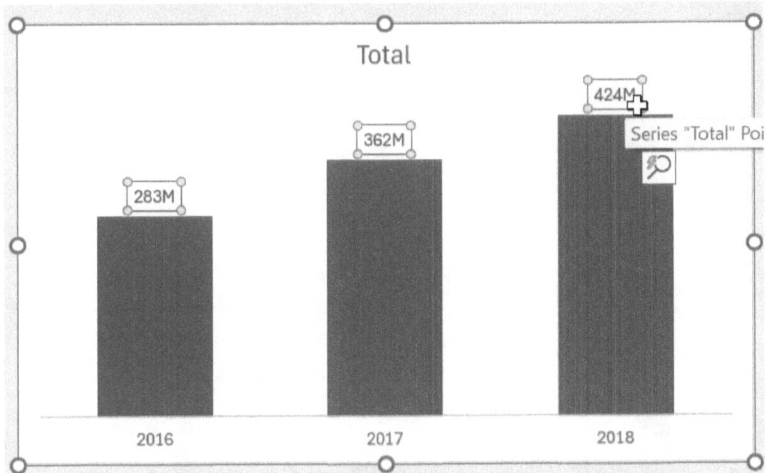

14. Go to the **Home** tab and change the **Font Size** to **12**.

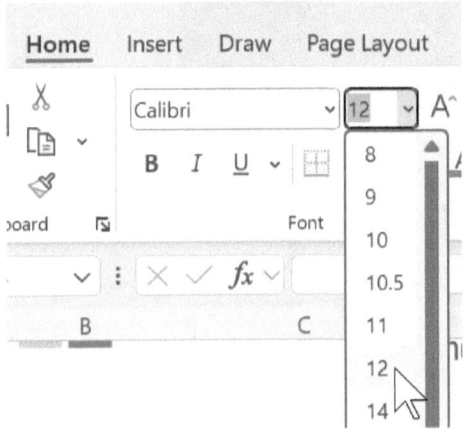

15. Click on the **Horizontal Axis** to select it. Change the **Font Size** to **12**.

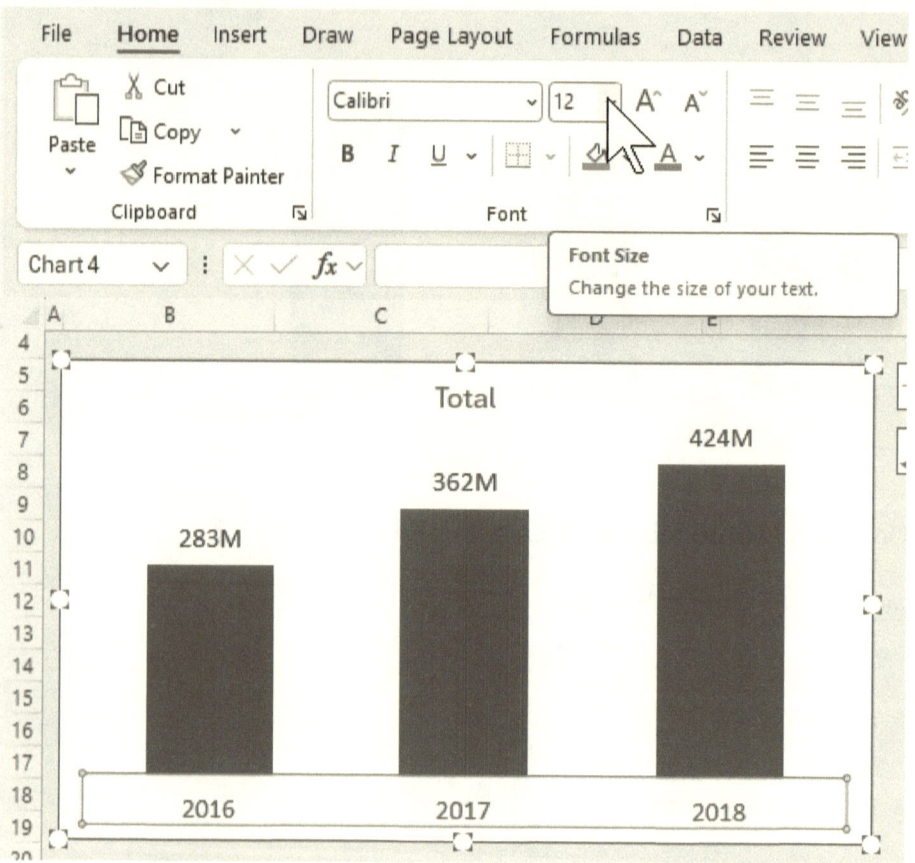

Creating (Power) PivotCharts

16. Double-click the **Chart Title** to edit it and type **Revenue by Year**.

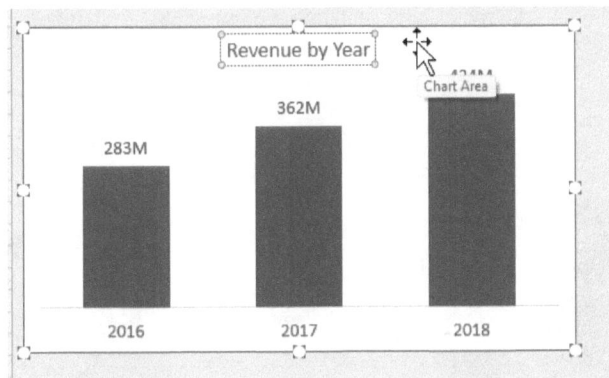

17. With the chart selected, go to **the Format tab, Shape Outline,** and click **No Outline**.

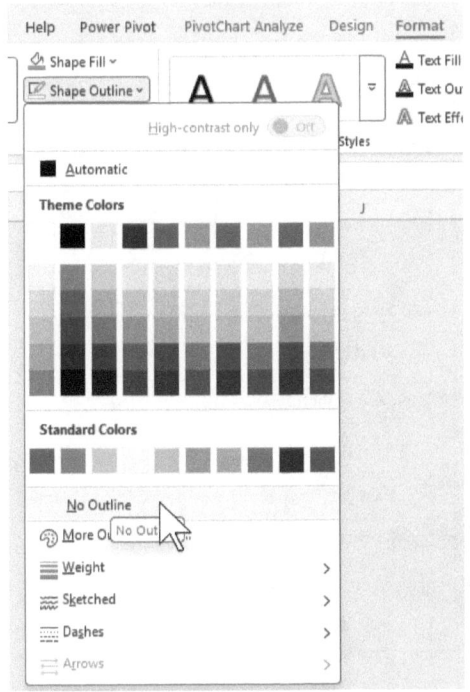

18. **Right-click** the chart area (the white background) and click on **PivotChart Options**.

64   Excel Power Suite – Business Intelligence Clinic

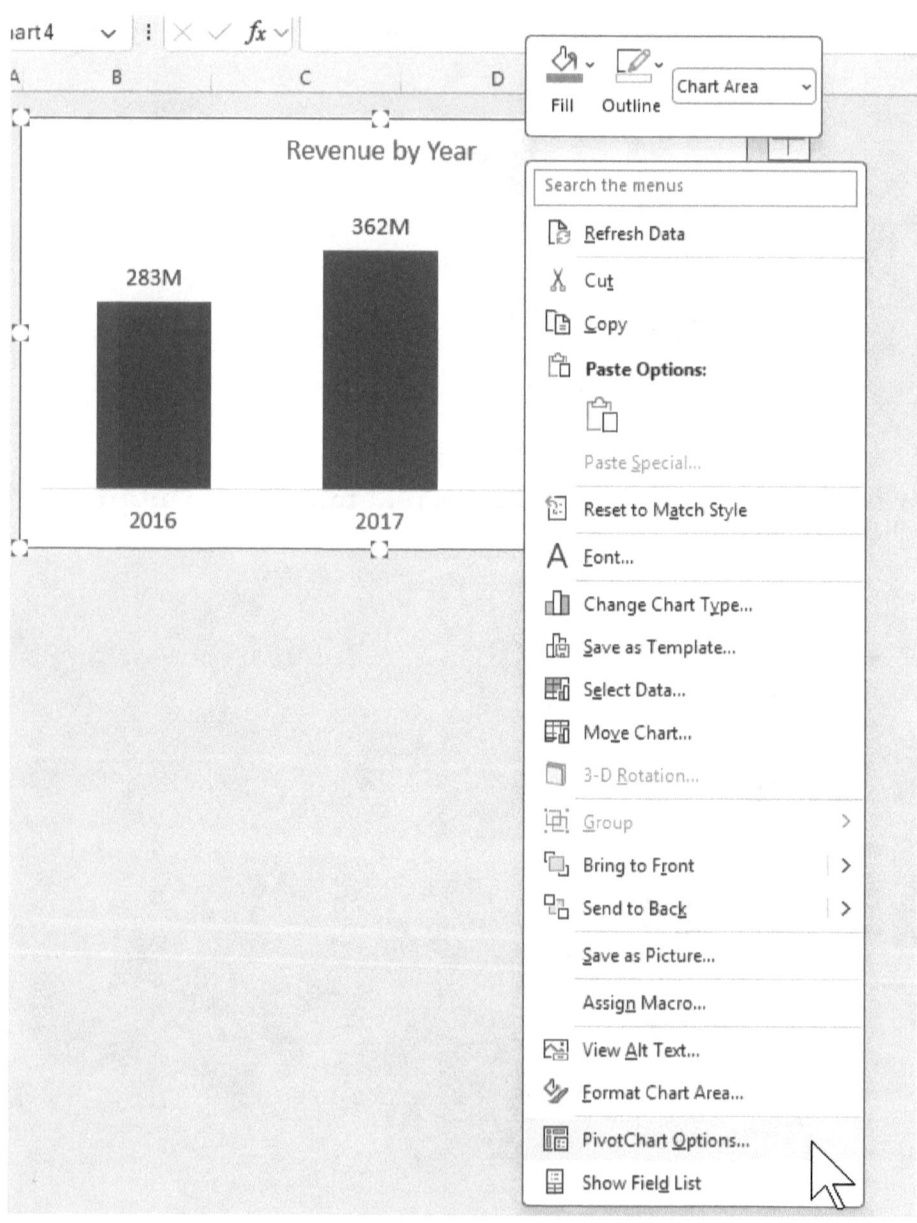

Creating (Power) PivotCharts

19. Change the **PivotChart Name** to **cRevenueByYear**. Then click **OK**.

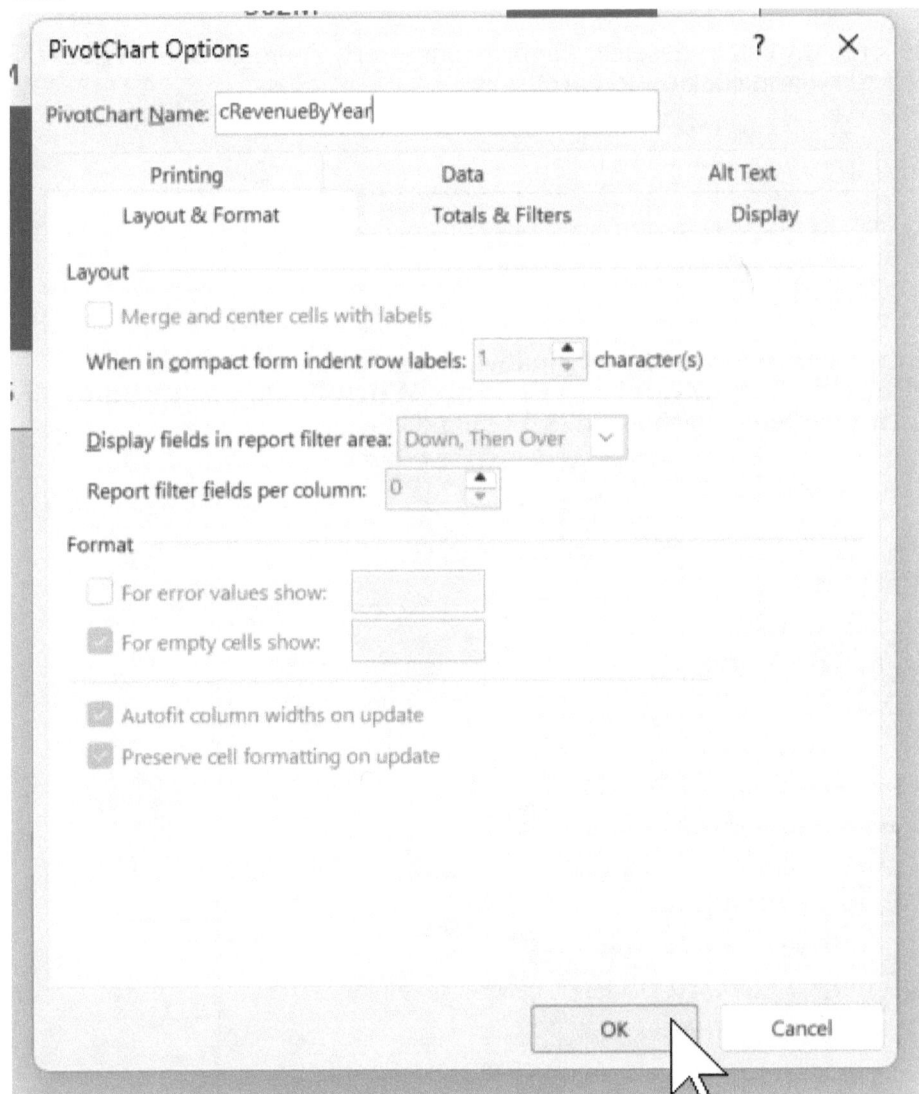

7. Doughnut Chart

1. Click on any cell to deselect the previous chart. Then, go to the **Insert** tab, **Charts**, and click on **PivotChart**.

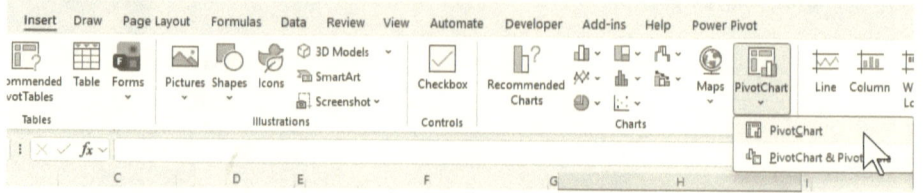

2. In the **Create PivotChart** window, check the item **Use this workbook's Data Model** and **Existing Worksheet**. Then set the **Location** as 'Sales Dashboard'!$B$25 and click **OK**.

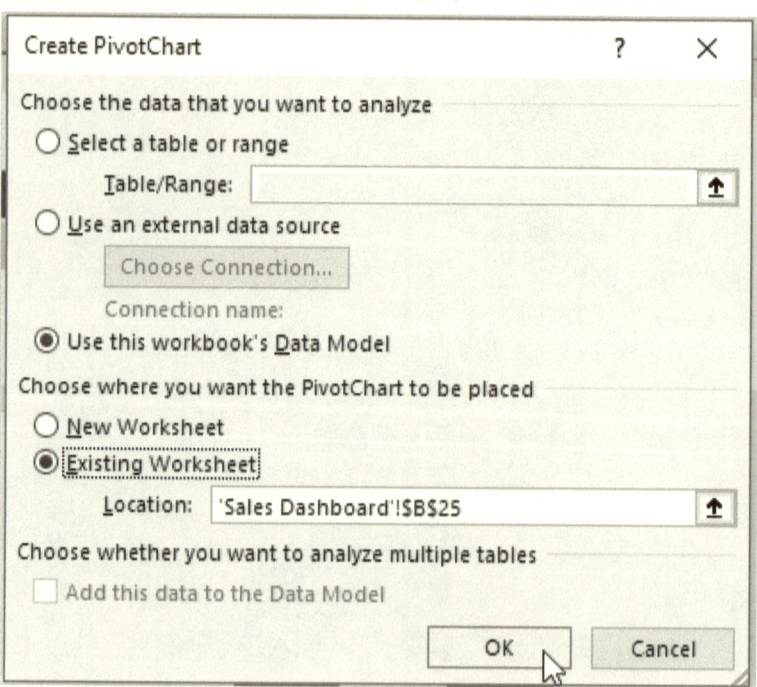

Creating (Power) PivotCharts

3. Add the field **Order method type** in the **Axis (Categories)** section and the field **Revenue** in the **Value** section. The fields can be moved by dragging and dropping or right-clicking and selecting the section.

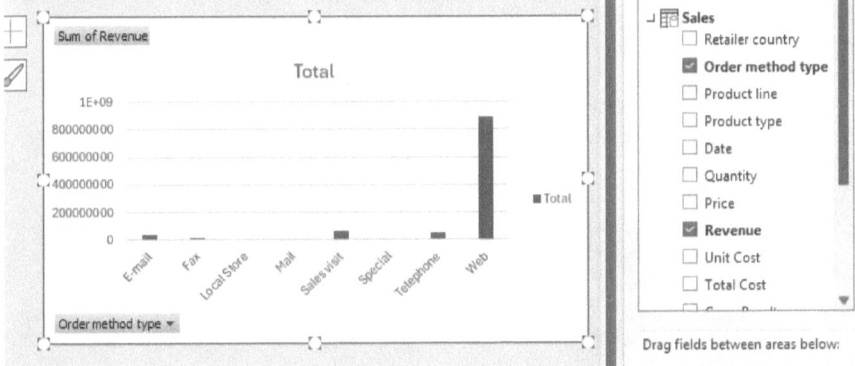

4. With the chart selected, go to the **Design** tab and click on **Change Chart Type**.

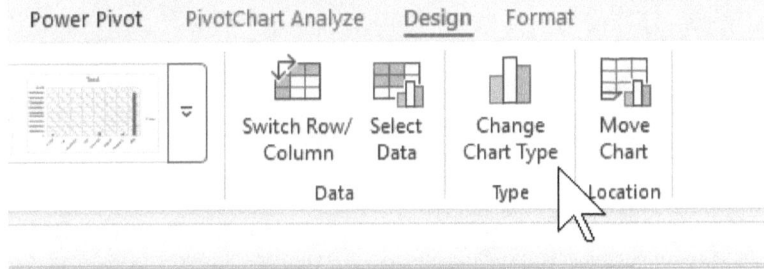

5. Go to **Pie** group, select **Doughnut**, and **OK**.

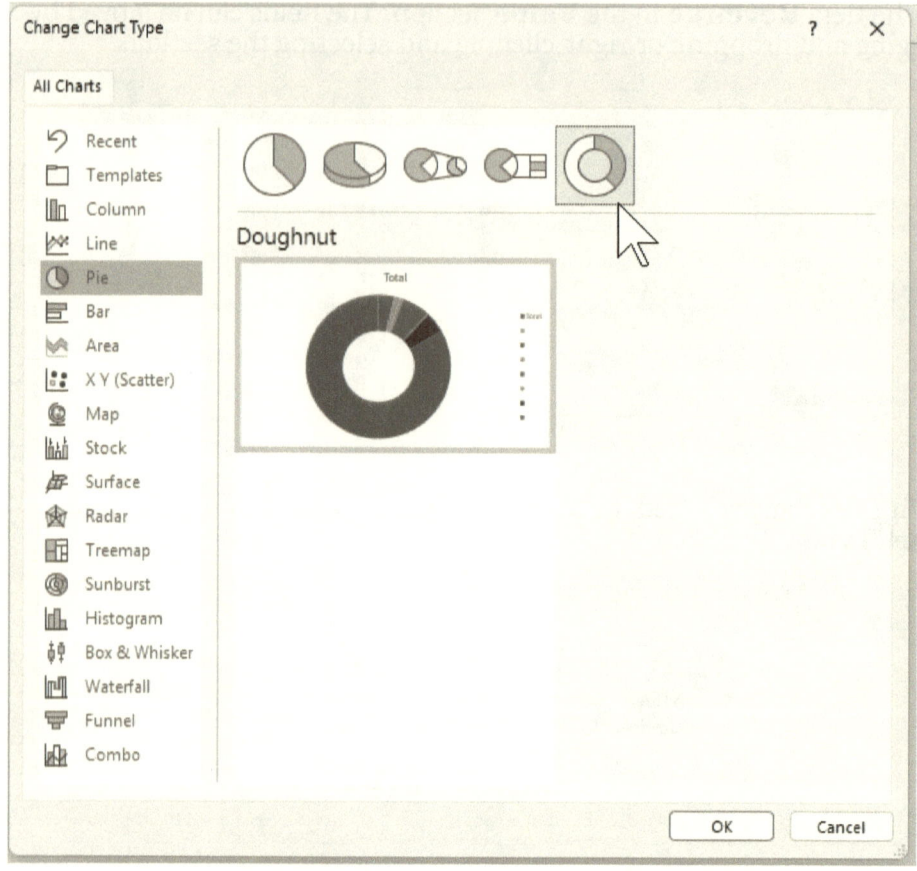

Creating (Power) PivotCharts

6. Go to the **PivotChart Analyze** tab, click **Field Buttons**, and select **Hide All**.

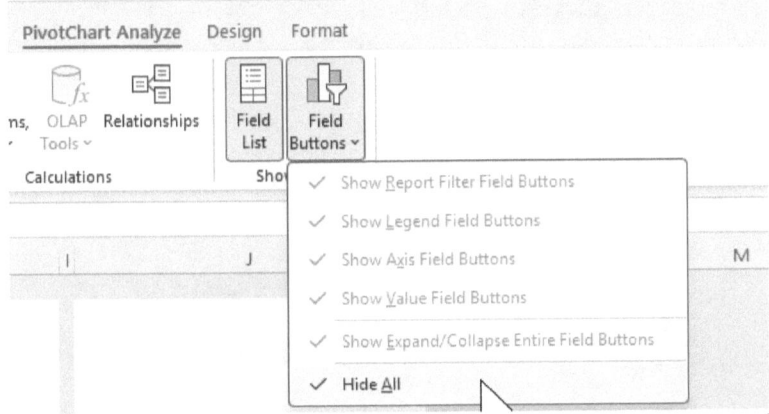

7. Right-click the **Doughnut Chart** and click on **Format Data Series**.

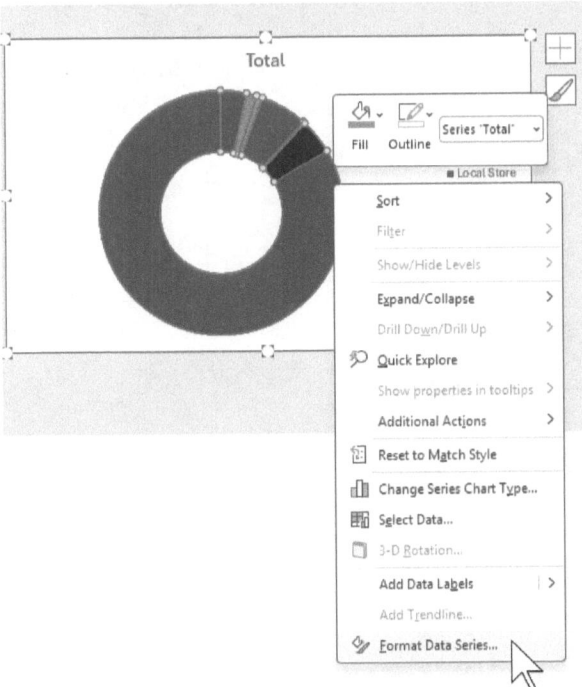

8. Go **to Series Options** and set the **Doughnut Hole Size** to 65%.

9. Click on **Chart Elements**, Legend, and select **Bottom**.

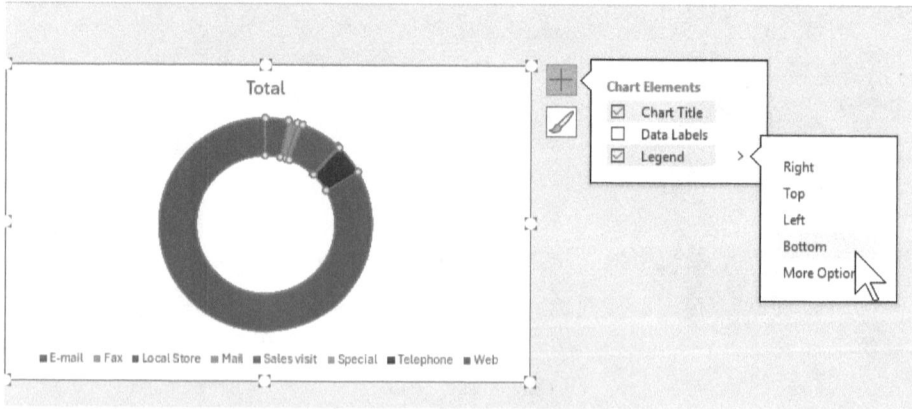

Creating (Power) PivotCharts

10. Click once on the Doughnut and click again on the largest category (**Web**) to select it. Right-click the **Web** category and change the **Shape Fill** color to **Green**.

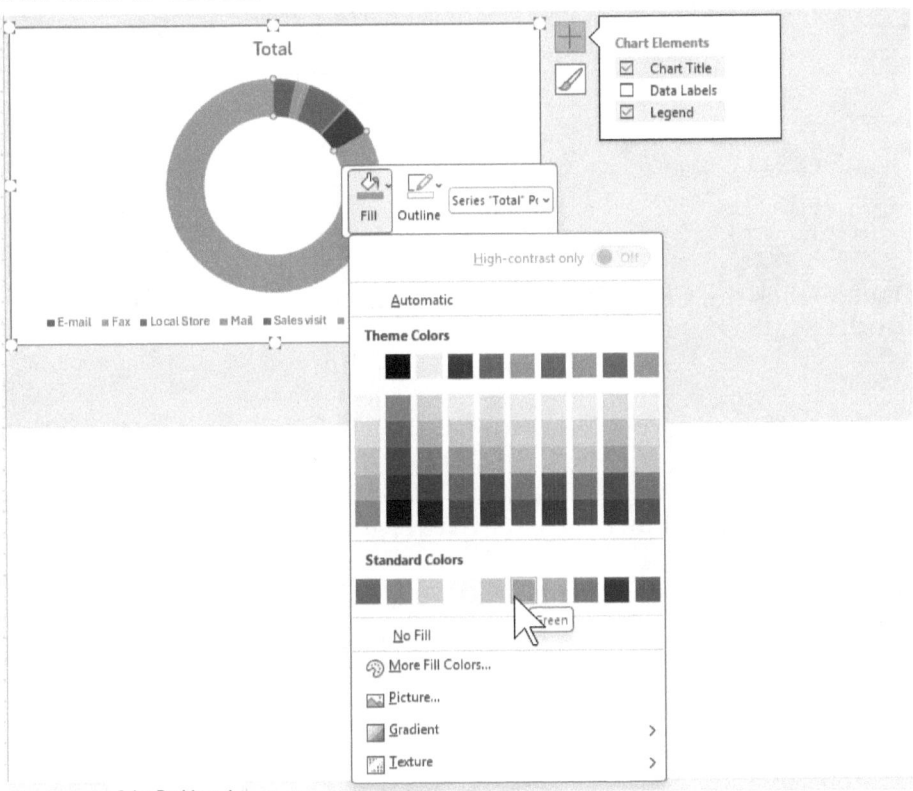

11. Click on **Chart Legend** to select it. Then go to the **Home** tab and change the **Font Size** to **10.5**.

12. Double-click the **Chart Title** to edit it and type **Revenue by Order Method**.

13. Go to the **Format** tab, **Shape Outline**, and click **No Outline**.

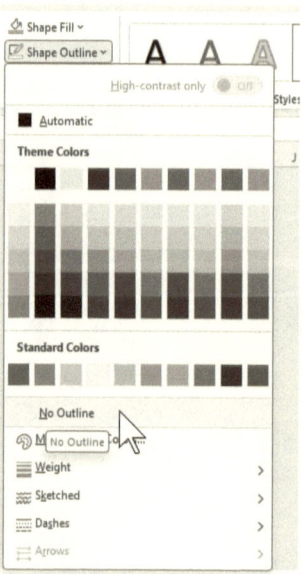

Creating (Power) PivotCharts

14. **Right-click** the chart area and click on **PivotChart Options**.

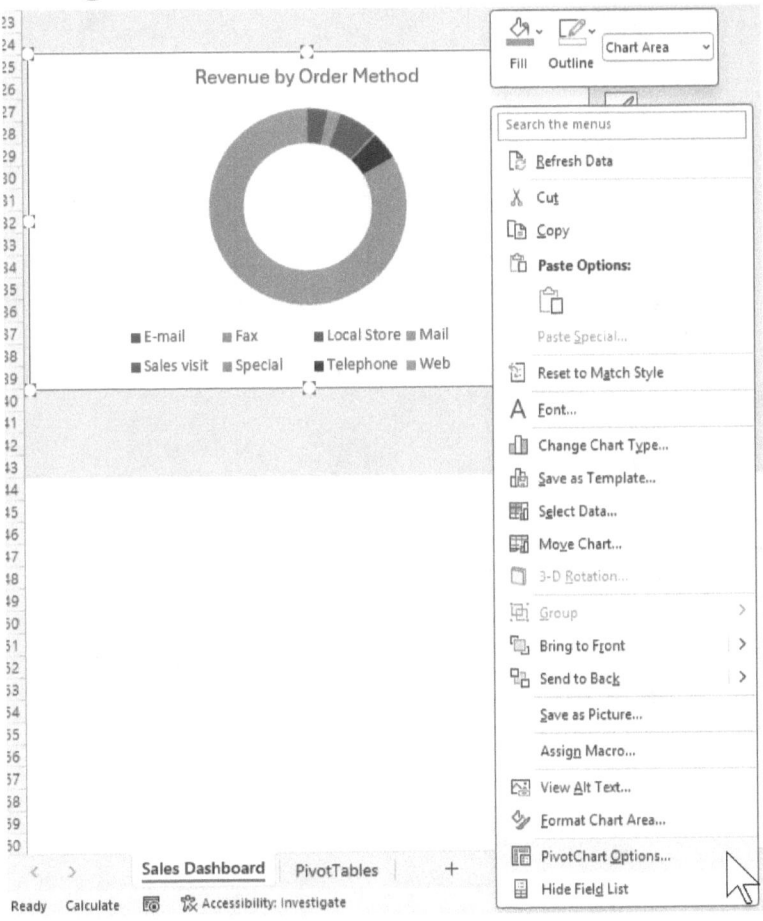

15. Change the PivotChart Name to **cRevenueByOrderMethod**. Then click **OK**.

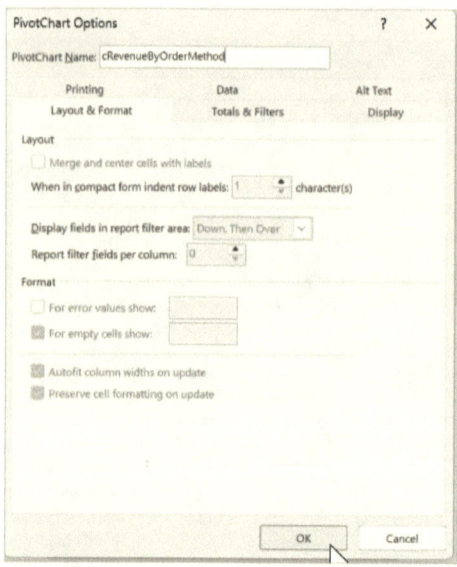

16. Drag and drop the charts to have a Dashboard similar to the image below.

Creating (Power) PivotCharts
75

8. Line Chart

1. Click on any cell to deselect the previous chart. Then, go to the **Insert** tab, **Charts**, and click on **PivotChart**.

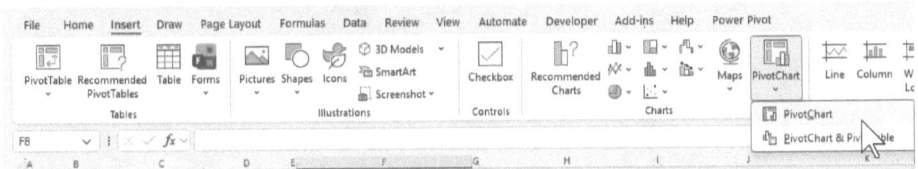

2. In the **Create PivotChart** window, check the item **Use this workbook's Data Model** and **Existing Worksheet**. Then set the **Location** as 'Sales Dashboard'!$F$5 and click **OK**.

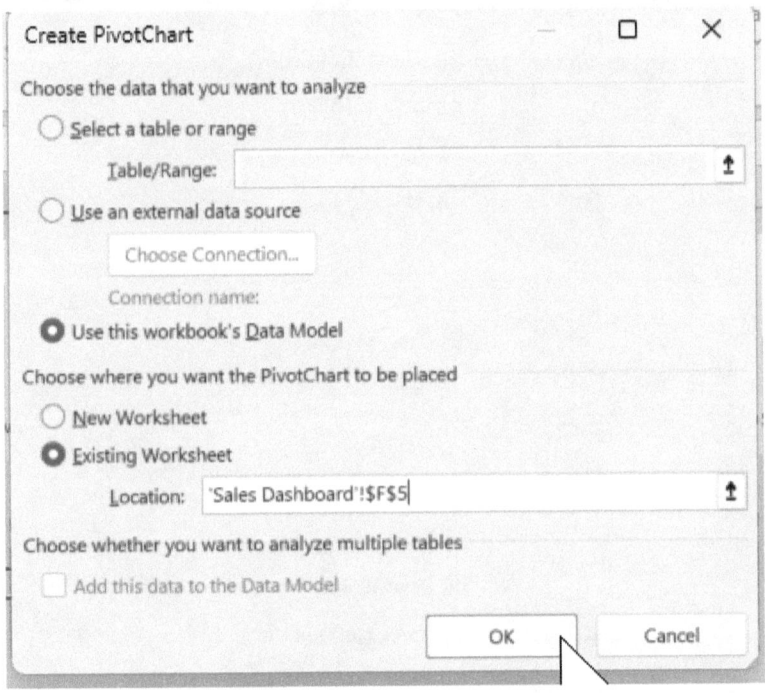

www.createandlearn.net

3. Right-Click the PivotChart area and click on **Show Field List**.

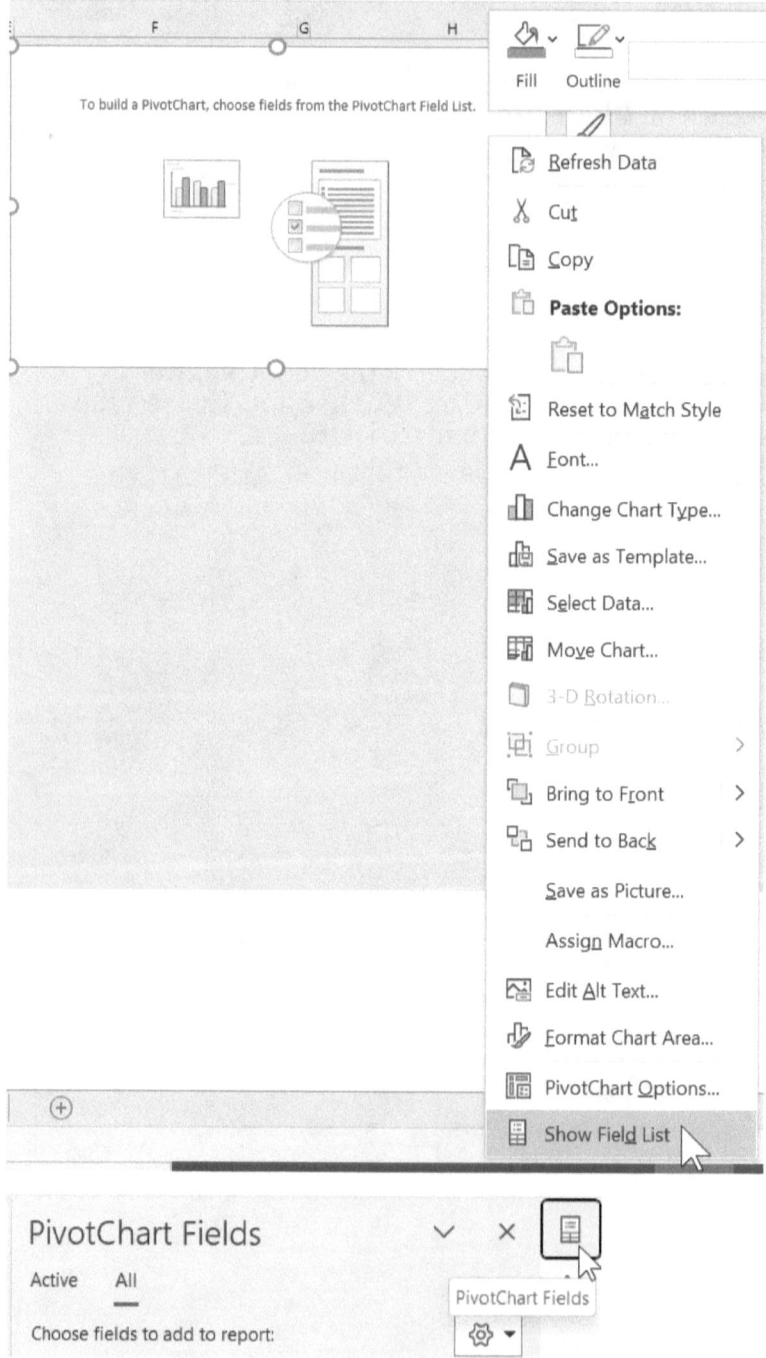

Creating (Power) PivotCharts

4. Add the field **Start of Month** in the **Axis (Categories)** section, the Region in the Legend (Series), and the Revenue field in the **Value** section. The fields can be moved by dragging and dropping or right-clicking and selecting the section.

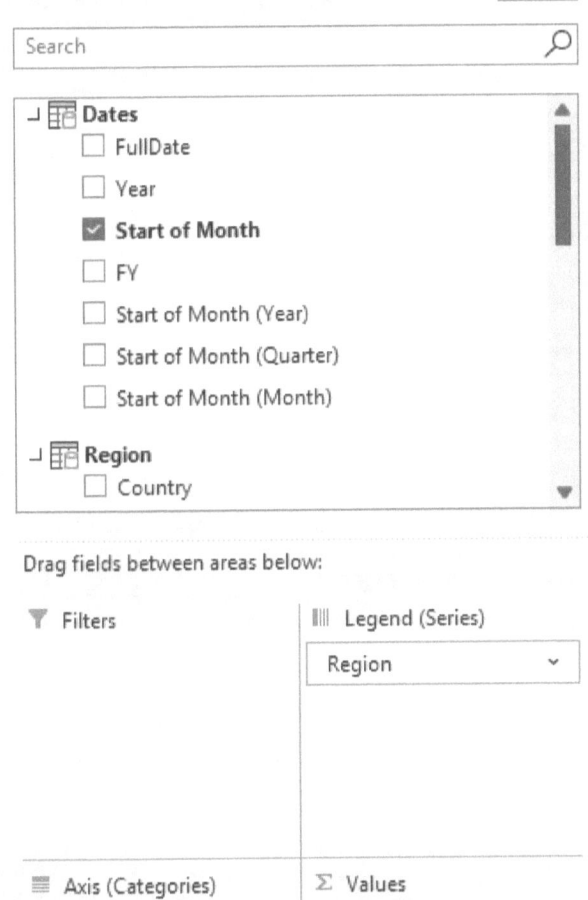

Remove any extra date category if needed.

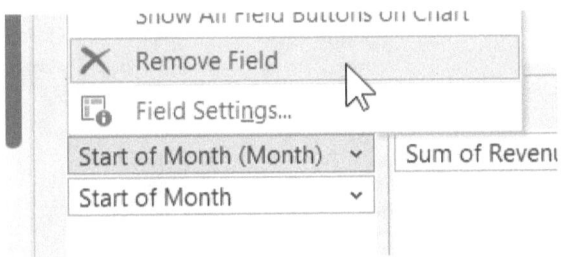

5. Go to the **PivotChart Analyze** tab, click on Field Buttons, and select **Hide All**.

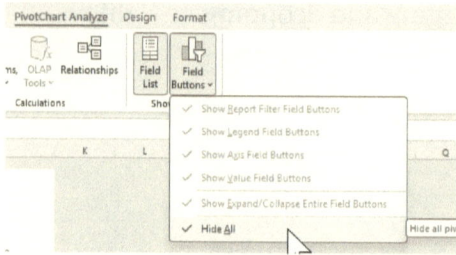

6. With the chart selected, go to the **Design** tab and click on **Change Chart Type**.

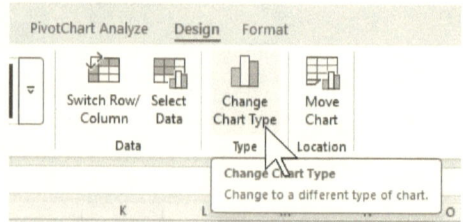

7. Go to **Line** group, select **Line**, and click **OK**.

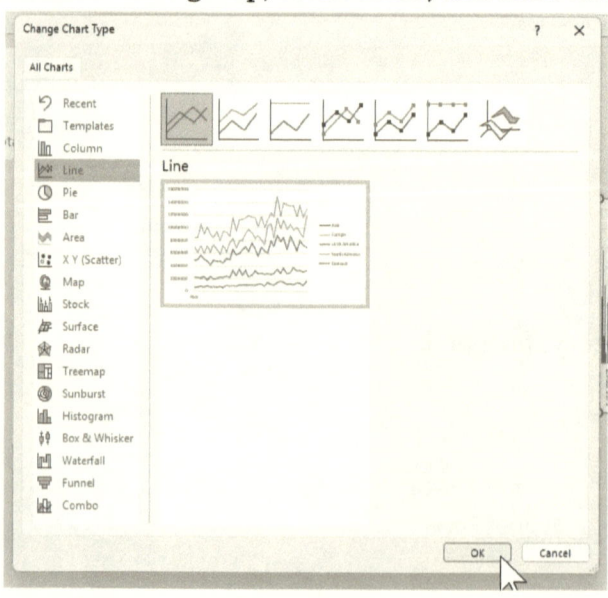

Creating (Power) PivotCharts

8. Go to **Chart Elements**, **Legend**, and click on **Top**.

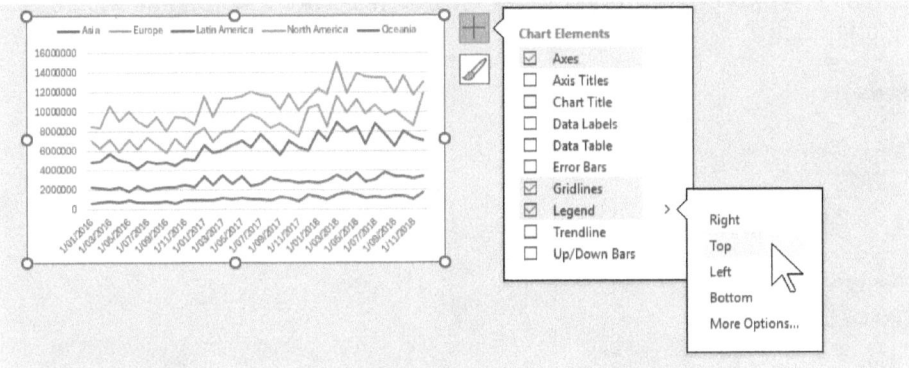

9. Right-click the **Vertical Axis** and click on **Format Axis**.

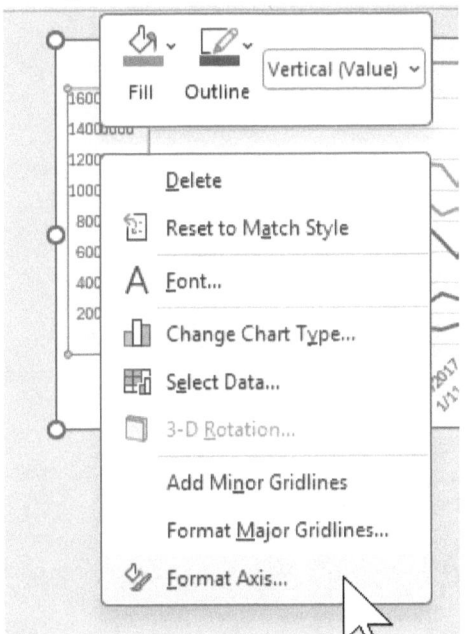

10. Go to **Axis Options**, **Number**, and change the **Category** to **Custom**. Then, type in the **Format Code** field the new format **#,,"M"**. Then, click Add.

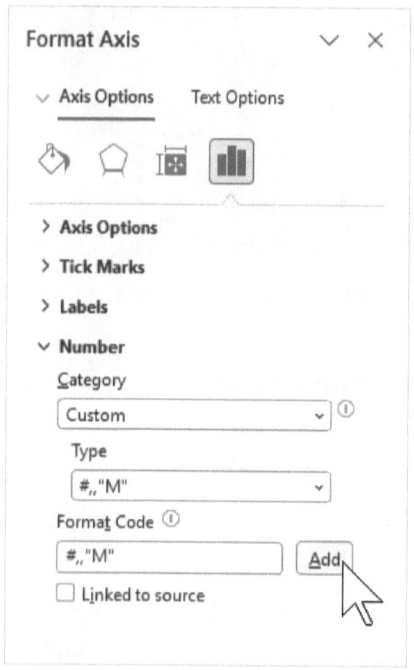

11. Click on **Chart Legend** to select it. Then, go to the **Home** tab and change the **Font Size** to **12**.

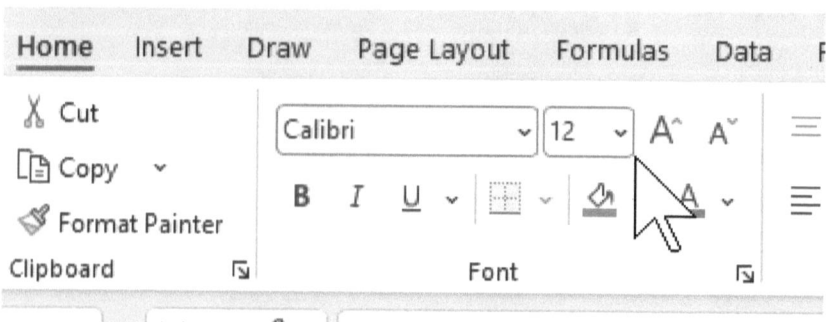

Creating (Power) PivotCharts   81

12. Select the chart area. Then, go to the **Format** tab, **Shape Outline**, and click **No Outline**.

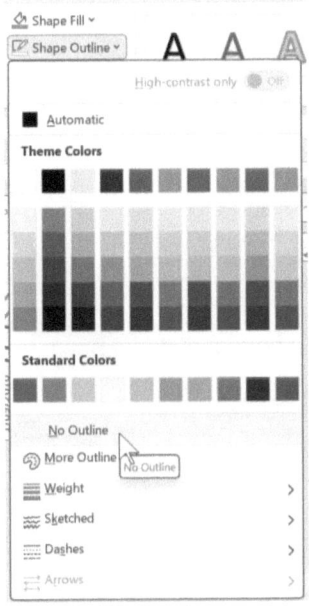

13. Click on **Chart Elements** and check the option **Chart Title**. Then, Double-click the chart title to edit, and type **Revenue by Month**.

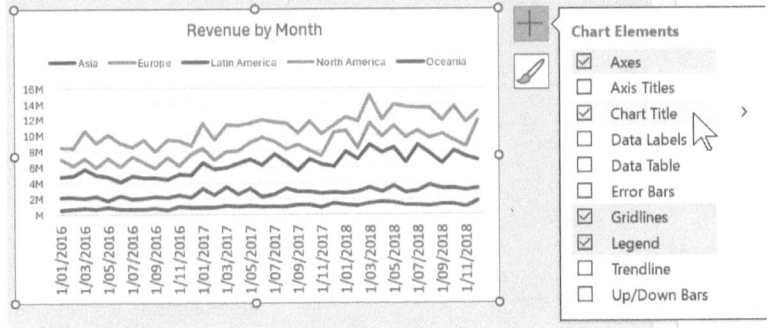

www.createandlearn.net

14. Right-click the chart area and click on **PivotChart Options**.

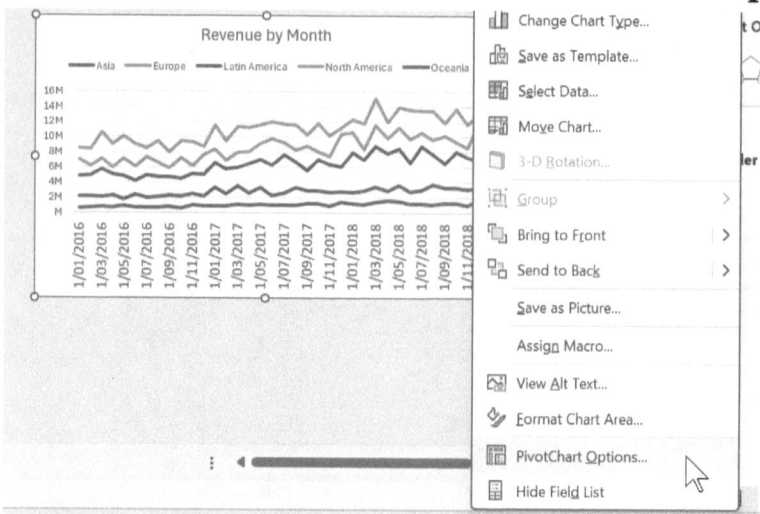

Creating (Power) PivotCharts

15. Change the PivotChart Name to **cMonthlyRevenue**. Then click **OK**.

16. Drag, drop, and resize the chart to have a Dashboard similar to the image below.

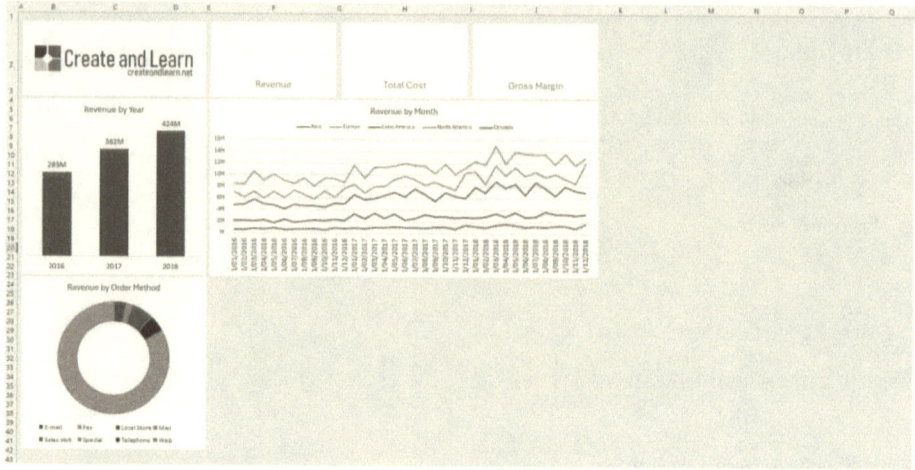

Creating (Power) PivotCharts   85

9. Stacked Bar

1. Go to the **Insert** tab, **Charts**, and click on **PivotChart**.

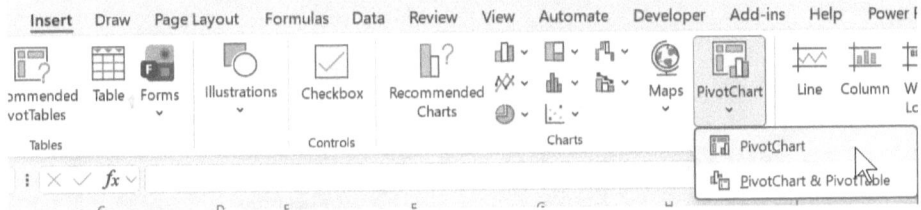

2. In the **Create PivotChart** window, check the item **Use this workbook's Data Model** and **Existing Worksheet**. Then set the **Location** as 'Sales Dashboard'!$F$24 and click **OK**.

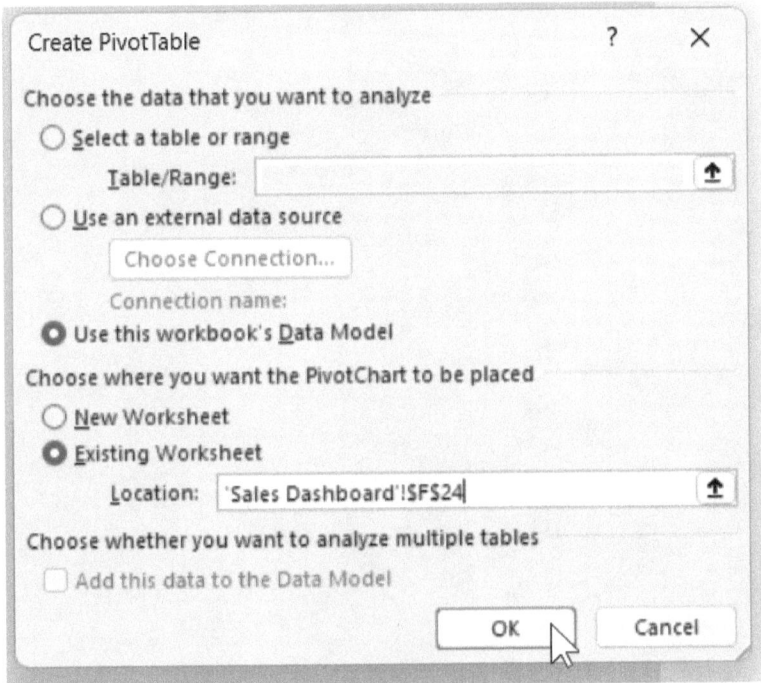

3. Right-click the PivotChart area and click on **Show Field List**.

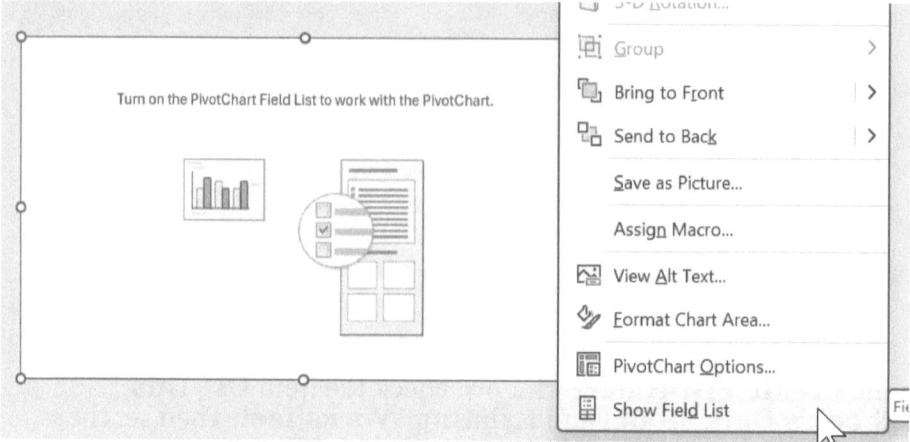

Creating (Power) PivotCharts

4. Add the field **Sales Manager** in the **Axis (Categories)** section, the field **Region** in the **Legend (Series)**, and the field **Revenue** in the **Value** section. The fields can be moved by dragging and dropping or right-clicking and selecting the section.

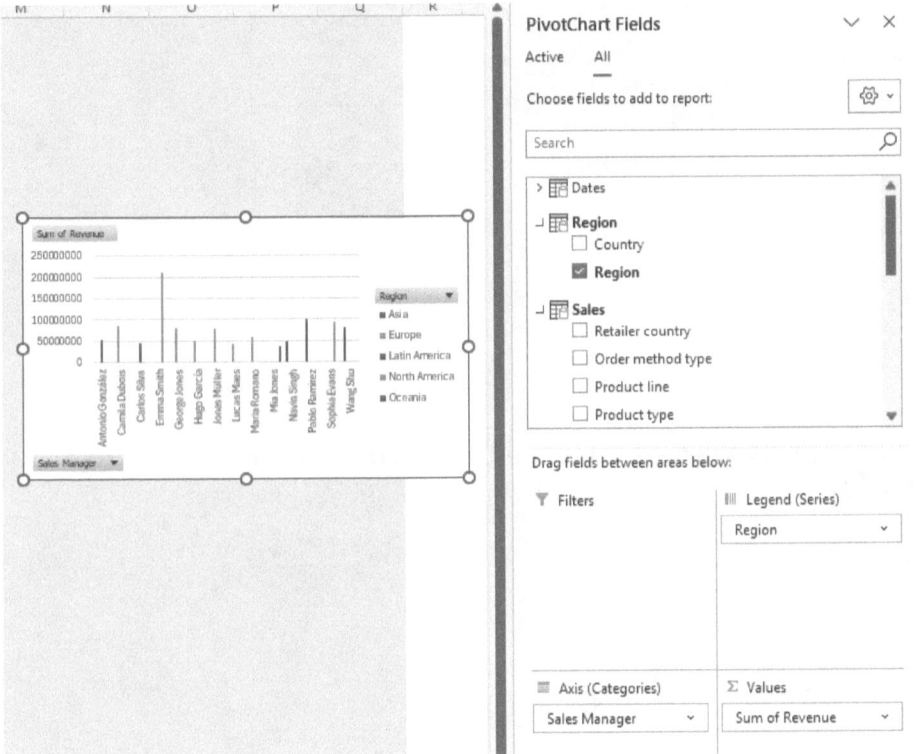

5. Go to the **PivotChart Analyze** tab, click on Field Buttons, and select **Hide All**.

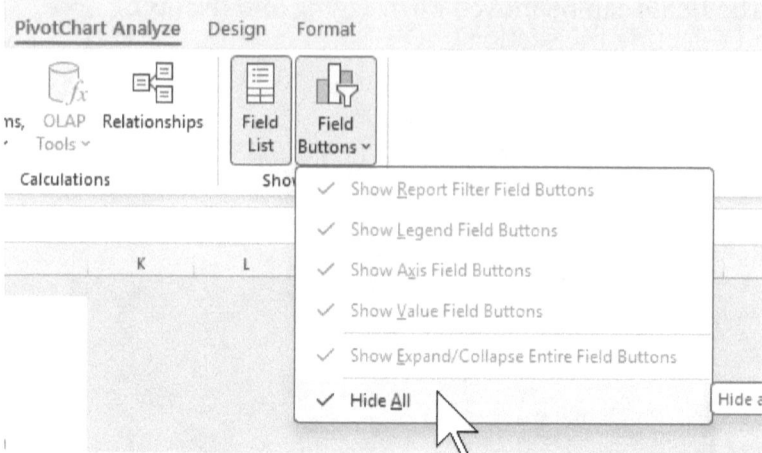

6. With the chart selected, go to the **Design** tab and click on **Change Chart Type**.

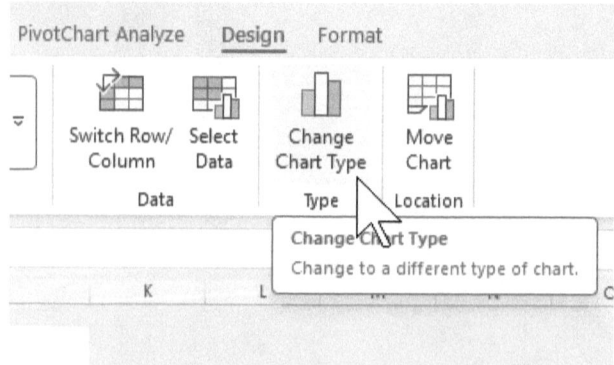

Creating (Power) PivotCharts

7. Go to **Bar** group, select **Stacked Bar**, and click **OK**.

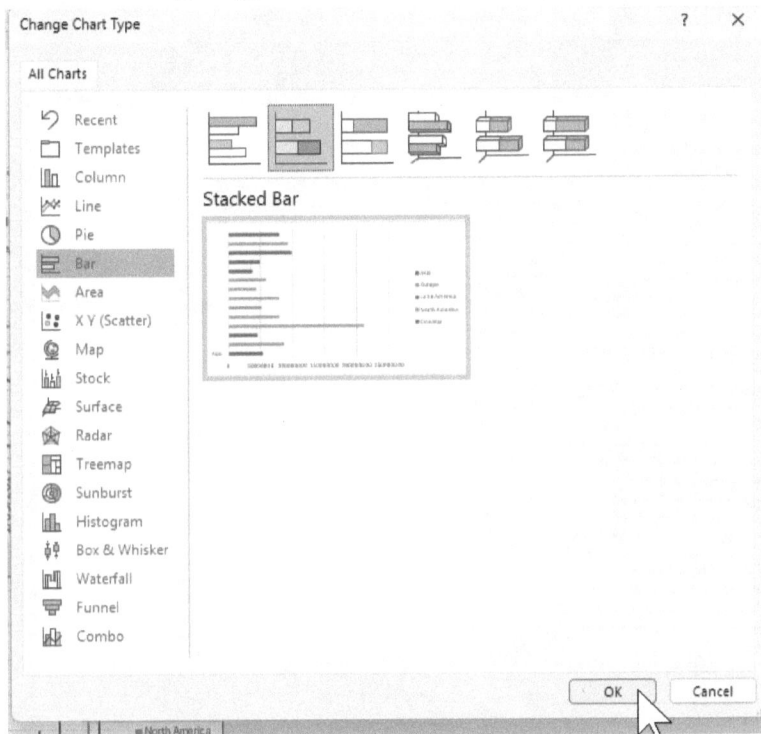

8. Go to **Chart Elements**, **Legend**, and click on **Top**.

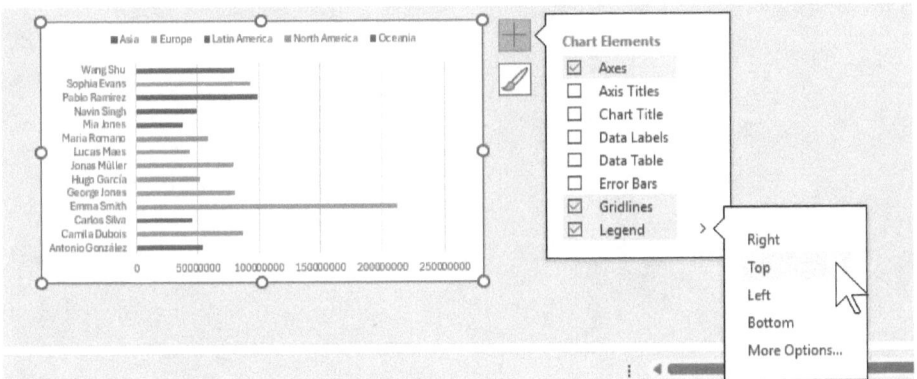

9. Right-click the **Horizontal Axis** and click on **Format Axis**.

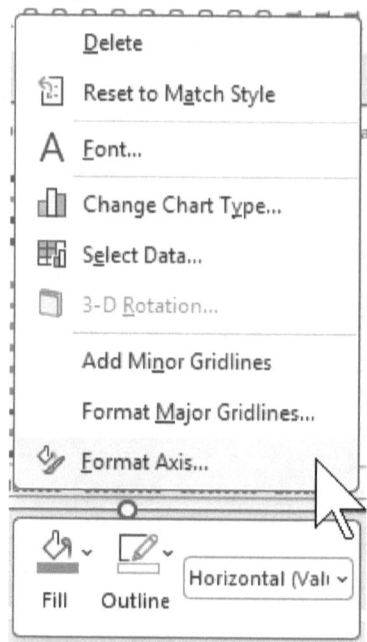

Creating (Power) PivotCharts

10. Go to **Axis Options**, **Number**, and change the **Category** to **Custom**. Then, type in the **Format Code** field the new format #,," M". Then, click Add.

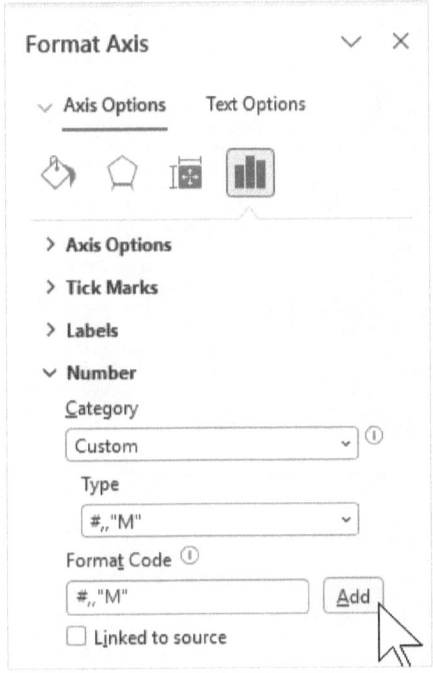

11. Right-click the **Vertical Axis**, go to **Sort**, and click on **More Sort Options**.

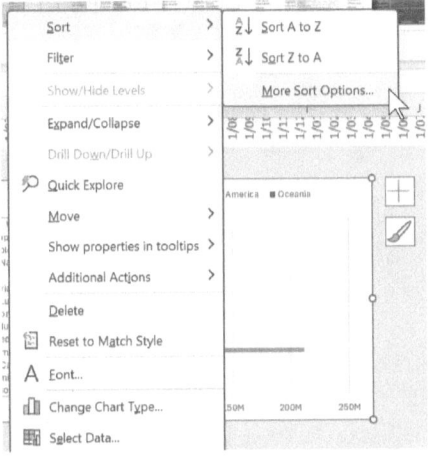

12. Check the option **Ascending (A to Z)** and select **Sum of Revenue**. Then, click **OK**.

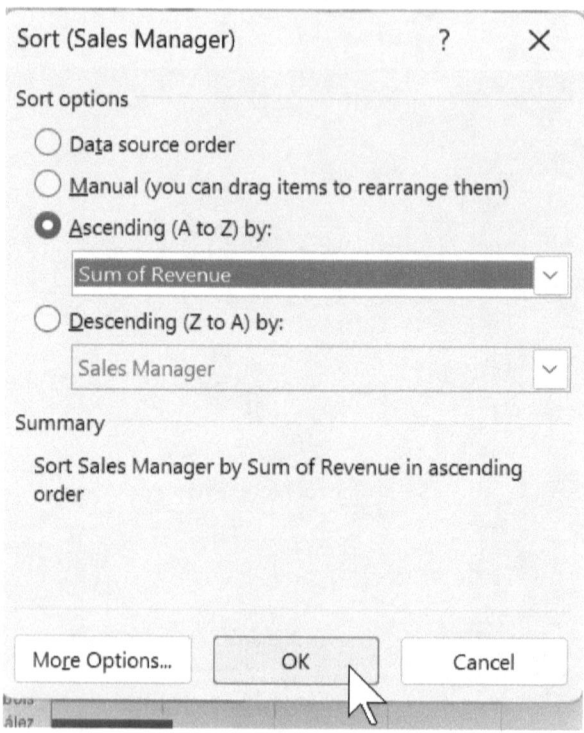

13. Click on the **Vertical Axis** and change the **Font Size** to 11.

14. Go to the **Format** tab, **Shape Outline**, and click **No Outline**.

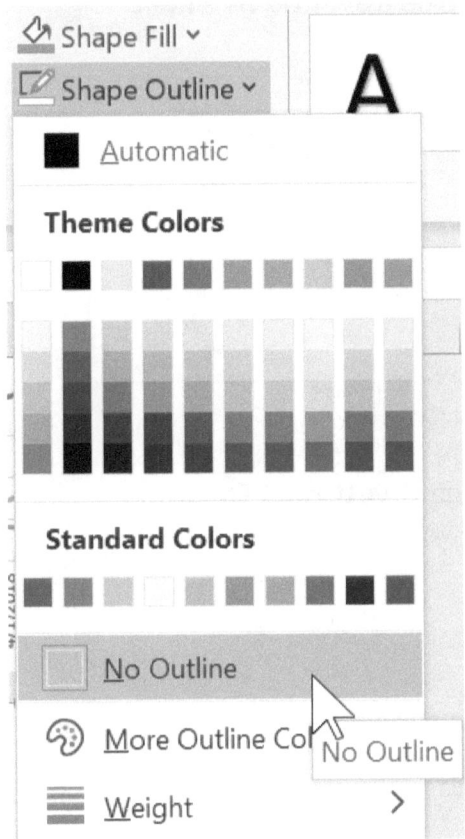

15. Click on **Chart Elements** and check the option **Chart Title**. Then, Double-click the chart title to edit, and type **Revenue by Sales Manager**.

16. Right-click the chart area and click on **PivotChart Options**.

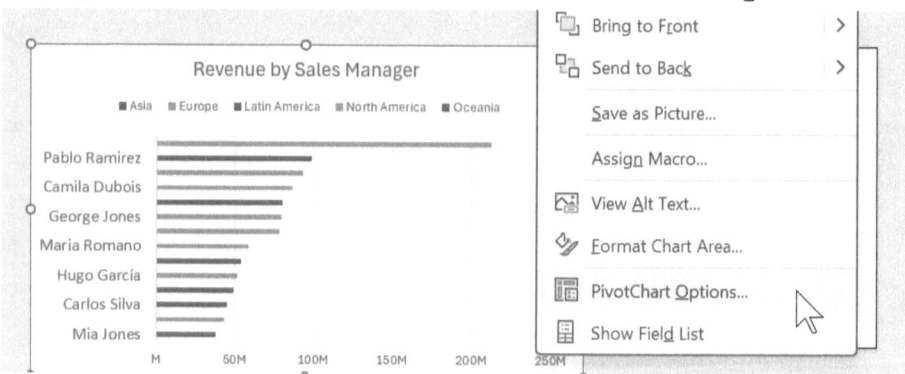

Creating (Power) PivotCharts

17. Change the PivotChart Name to **cRevenueBySalesManager**. Then click **OK**.

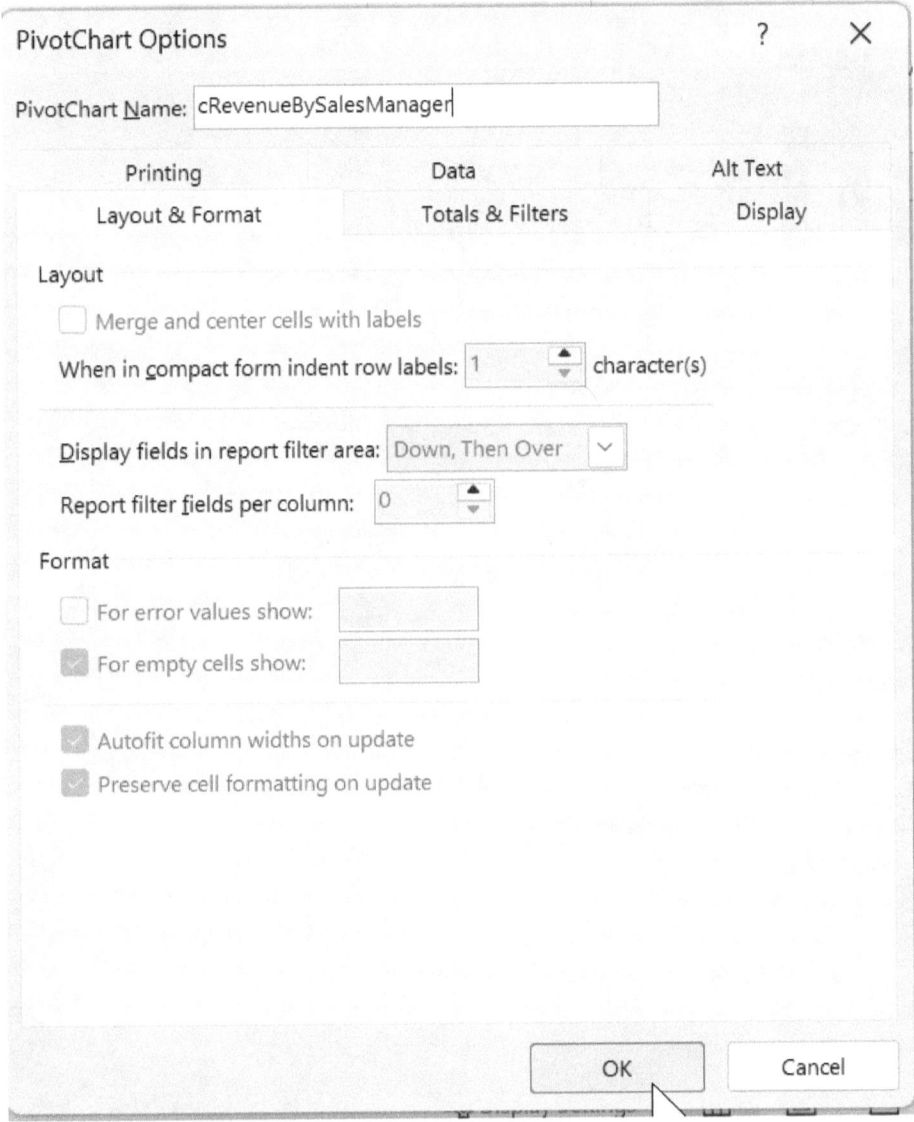

18. Drag, drop, and resize the chart to have a Dashboard similar to the image below.

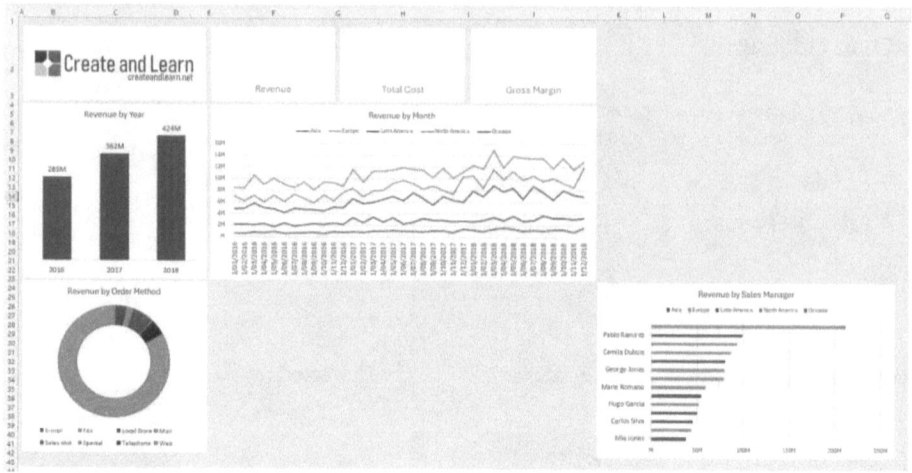

Chapter 5
Creating (Power) Pivot Tables

Power Pivot describes a standard **PivotTable** that can access the whole data model, allowing the user to create a PivotTable using data from the **Data Model** tool, containing multiple sources and custom calculations.

10. PivotTable Revenue By Product Line

1. Click on the **PivotTables** tab.

2. Select cell **A1**, go to **Insert**, **PivotTable**, and select **From Data Model**.

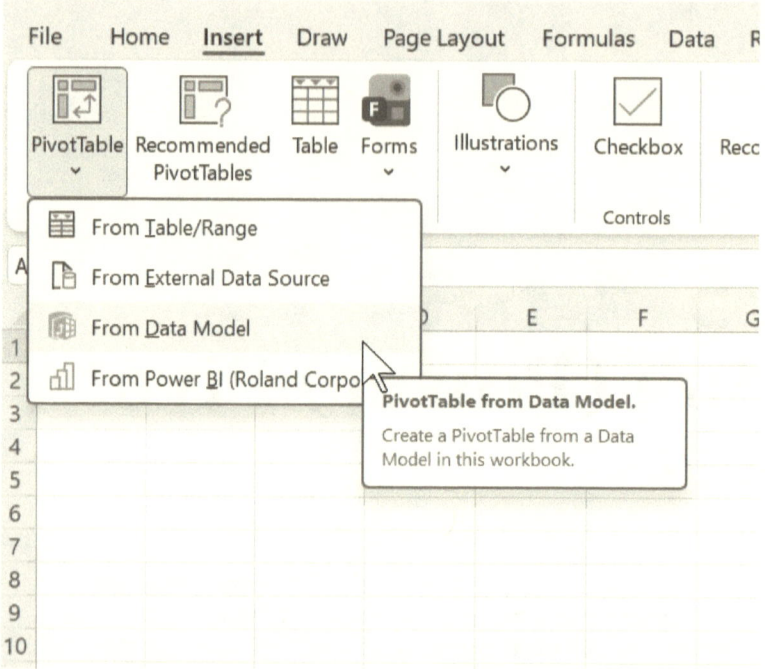

3. In the **PivotTable from Data Model** window, check the item **Existing Worksheet**. Then set the **Location** as **PivotTables!$A$1** and click **OK**.

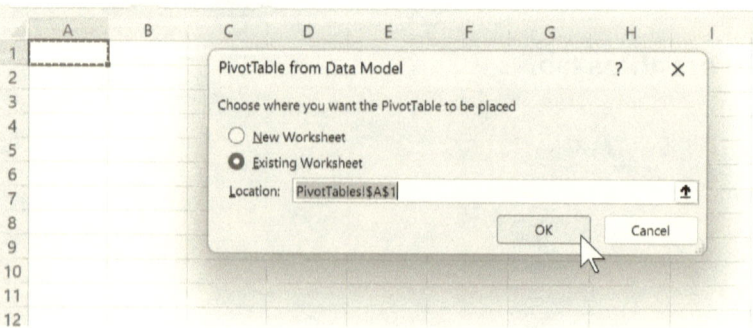

Creating (Power) Pivot Tables

99

4. Add the field **Product line**, Product type in the Rows section, and **Revenue** in the **Values** section. If needed, right-click the PivotChart area and click on **Show Field List**.

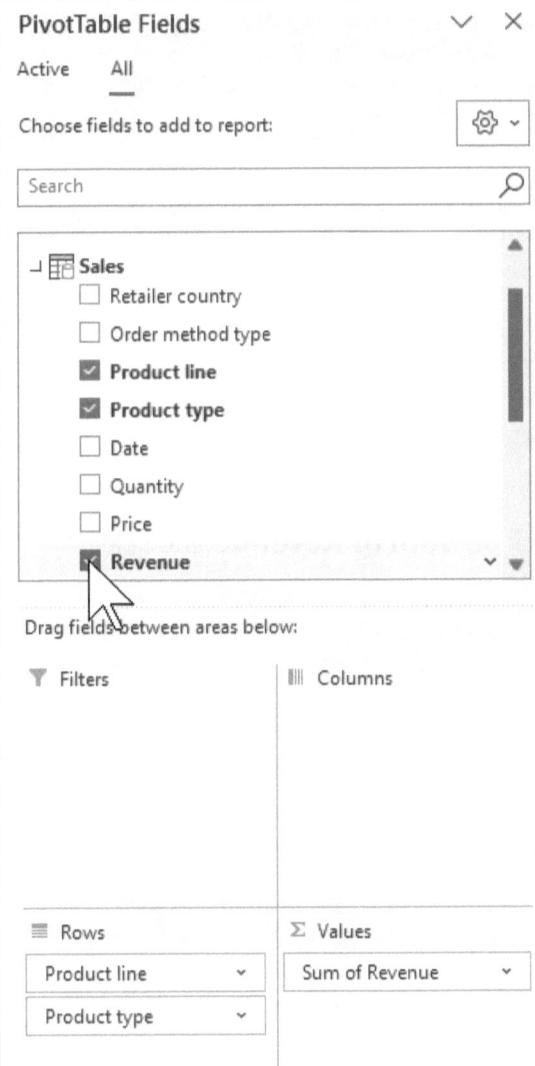

www.createandlearn.net

5. Go to the **Design** tab, **Report Layout**, and click on **Show in Tabular Form**.

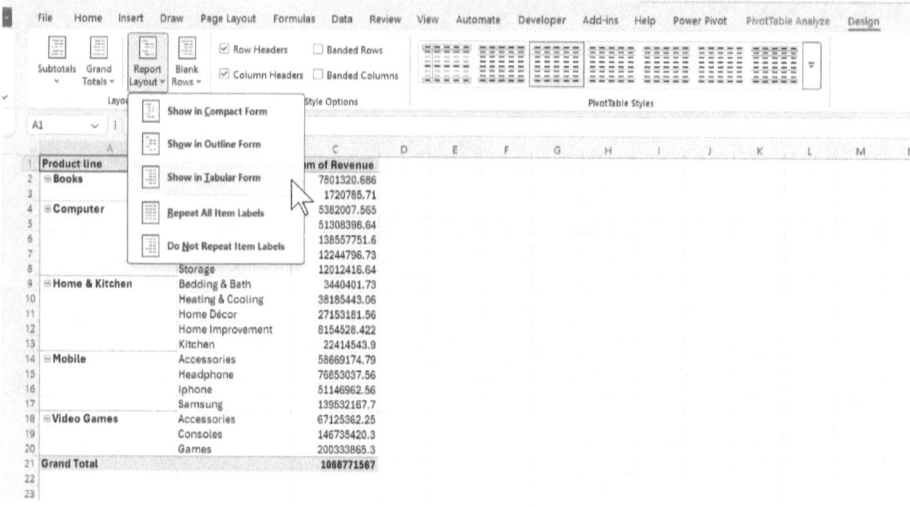

6. At the **PivotTable Fields**, click on **Sum of Revenue** and select **Value Field Settings**.

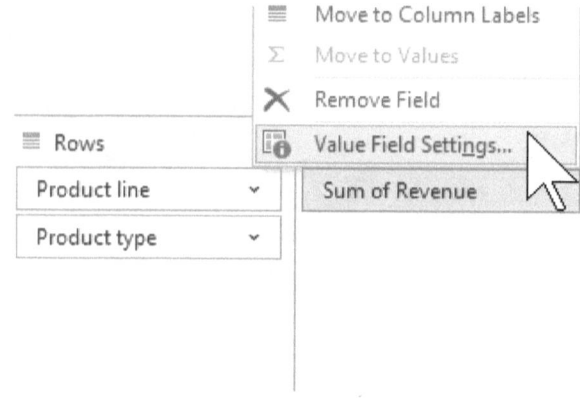

Creating (Power) Pivot Tables   101

7. In the **Value Field Settings** window, click on **Number Format**.

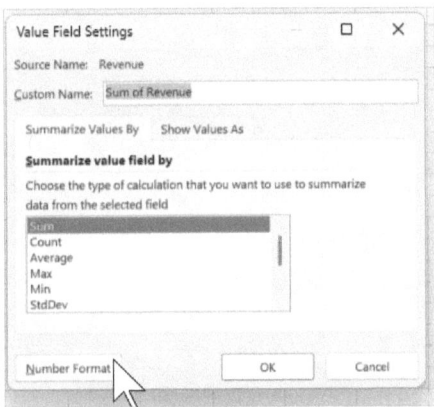

8. Select the **Number** category, set Decimal places to **Zero**, and check the option **Use 1000 Separator**. Then, click **OK** and **OK** again.

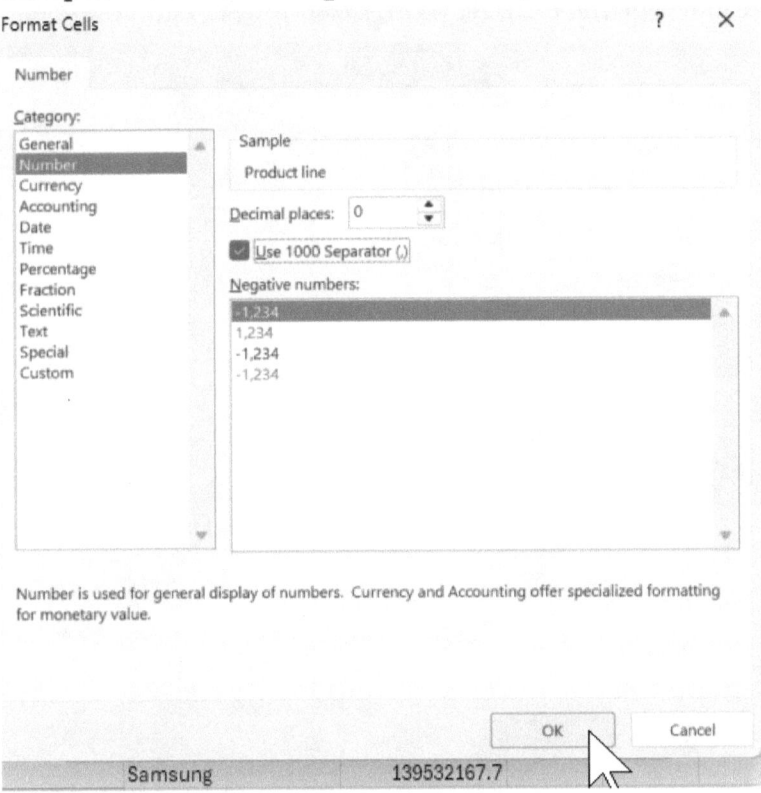

9. Go to the **Design** tab, **Grand Totals**, and select **Off for Rows and Columnns**.

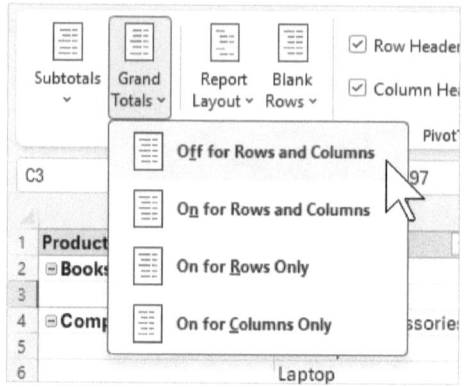

10. Select cell **G1** and type the formula **=IF(A1="","",A1)** and press **Enter**.

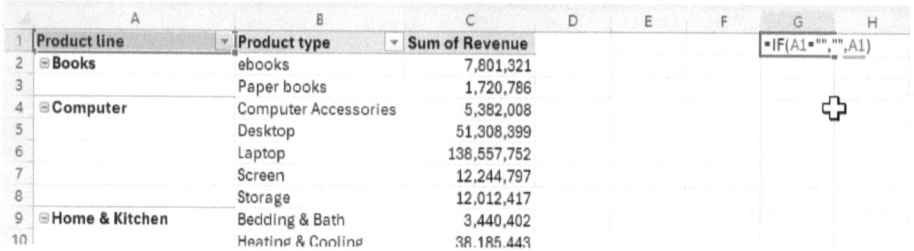

Creating (Power) Pivot Tables

11. Select cell **G1** and rest the cursor in the lower-right corner so that it turns into a plus sign **(+)**. Then, click and drag till cell **I1**, and drag to **I20**. After you drop it, the formula will be copied to every cell in the range **G1:I20**.

G	H	I
Product line	Product type	Sum of Revenue

G	H	I
Product line	Product type	Sum of Revenue
Books	ebooks	7801320.686
	Paper books	1720785.71
Computer	Computer Ac	5382007.565
	Desktop	51308398.64
	Laptop	138557751.6
	Screen	12244796.73
	Storage	12012416.64
Home & Kitch	Bedding & Ba	3440401.73
	Heating & Co	38185443.06
	Home Décor	27153181.56
	Home Improv	8154528.422
	Kitchen	22414543.9
Mobile	Accessories	58669174.79
	Headphone	76853037.56
	Iphone	51146962.56
	Samsung	139532167.7
Video Games	Accessories	67125362.25
	Consoles	146735420.3
	Games	200333865.3

12. Select range **I2:I20**. Then, right-click the selection and click on **Format Cells.**

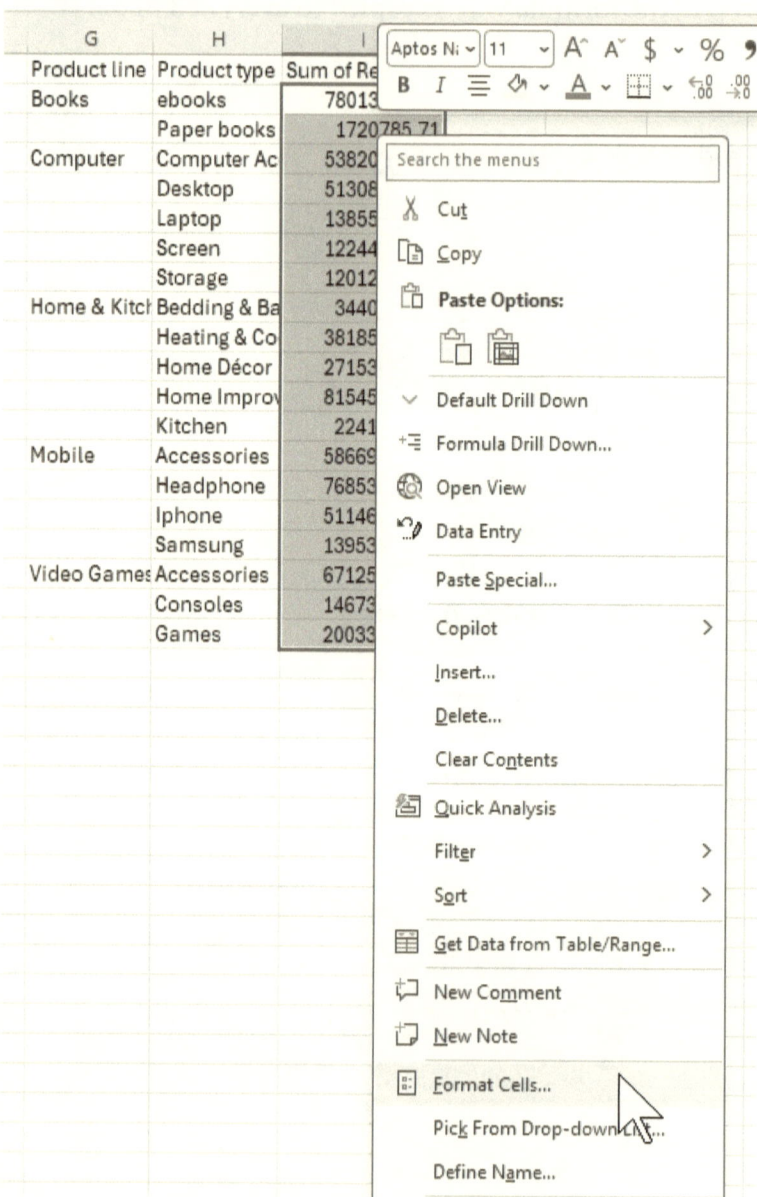

Creating (Power) Pivot Tables

13. In the **Format Cells** window, go to **Number**, **Custom**, and type the format **#0,, "M"**. Then, click **OK**.

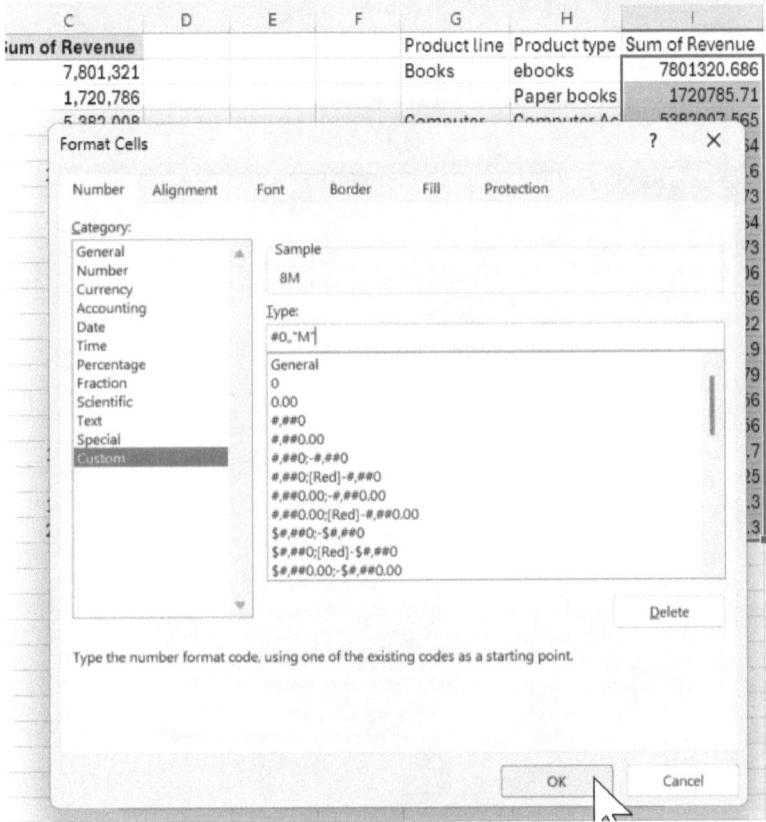

14. Right-click the PivotTable and click on **PivotTable Options**.

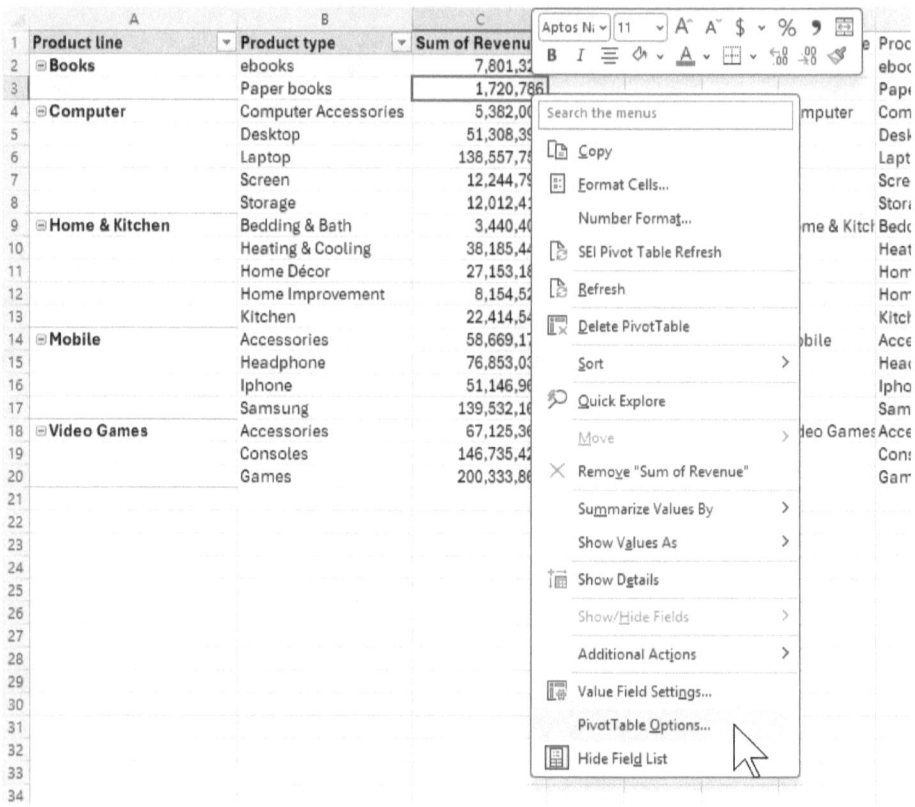

Creating (Power) Pivot Tables

15. Change the PivotTable Name field to **tRevenueByProductLine**.

16. The result should be like the image below.

Product line	Product type	Sum of Revenue					Product line	Product type	Sum of Revenue
⊟ Books	ebooks	7,801,321					Books	ebooks	8M
	Paper books	1,720,786						Paper books	2M
⊟ Computer	Computer Accessories	5,382,008					Computer	Computer Ac	5M
	Desktop	51,308,399						Desktop	51M
	Laptop	138,557,752						Laptop	139M
	Screen	12,244,797						Screen	12M
	Storage	12,012,417						Storage	12M
⊟ Home & Kitchen	Bedding & Bath	3,440,402					Home & Kitch	Bedding & Bat	3M
	Heating & Cooling	38,185,443						Heating & Co	38M
	Home Décor	27,153,182						Home Décor	27M
	Home Improvement	8,154,528						Home Improv	8M
	Kitchen	22,414,544						Kitchen	22M
⊟ Mobile	Accessories	58,669,175					Mobile	Accessories	59M
	Headphone	76,853,038						Headphone	77M
	Iphone	51,146,963						Iphone	51M
	Samsung	139,532,168						Samsung	140M
⊟ Video Games	Accessories	67,125,362					Video Games	Accessories	67M
	Consoles	146,735,420						Consoles	147M
	Games	200,333,865						Games	200M

11. PivotTable Revenue

1. Select cell **L1**, go to **Insert**, **PivotTable**, and select **From Data Model**.

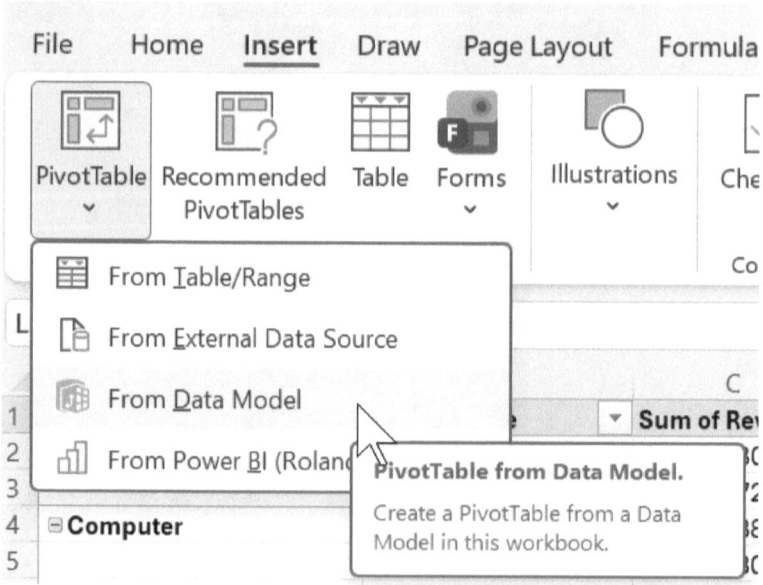

Creating (Power) Pivot Tables

2. In the **PivotTable from Data Model** window, check the item **Existing Worksheet**. Then set the **Location** as **PivotTables!$L$1** and click **OK**.

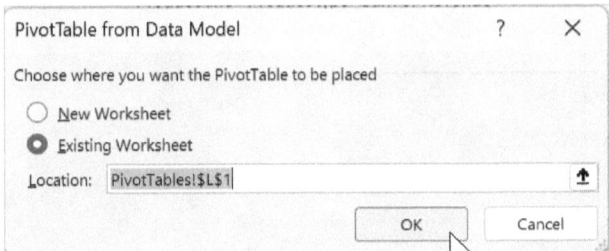

3. Add the **Revenue** field to the **Value** section.

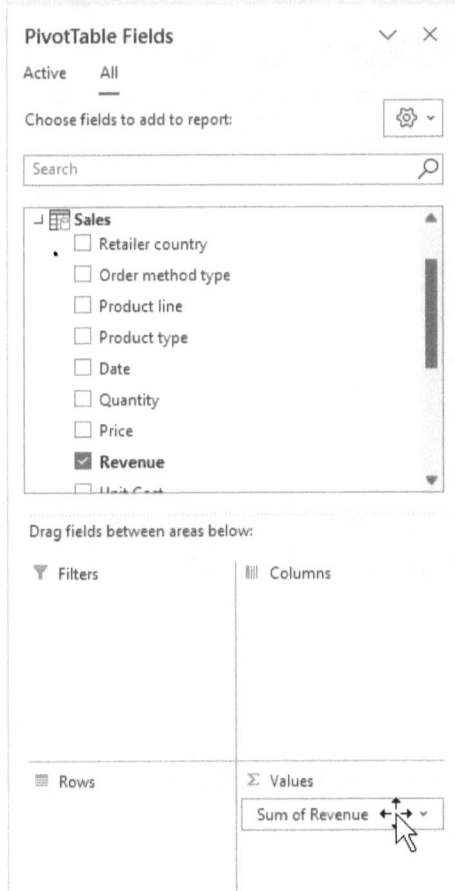

4. In the **PivotTable Fields**, click on **Sum of Revenue** and select **Value Field Settings**.

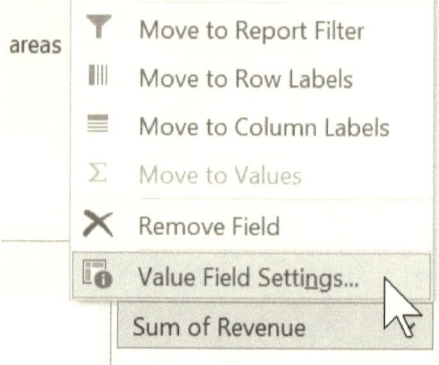

5. In the Value Field Settings window, click on **Number Format**.

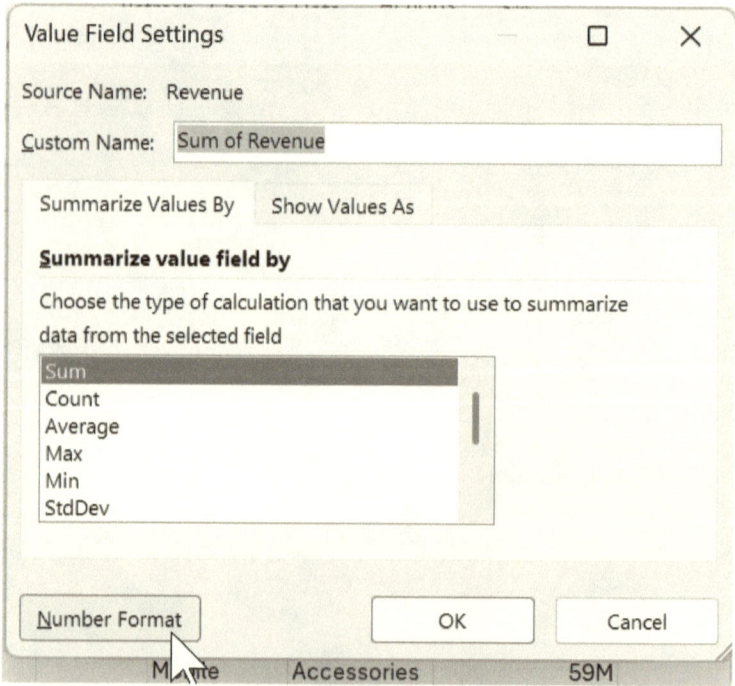

Creating (Power) Pivot Tables 111

6. In the **Format Cells** window, go to **Number**, **Custom**, and type the format **#0,, "M"**. Then click **OK**.

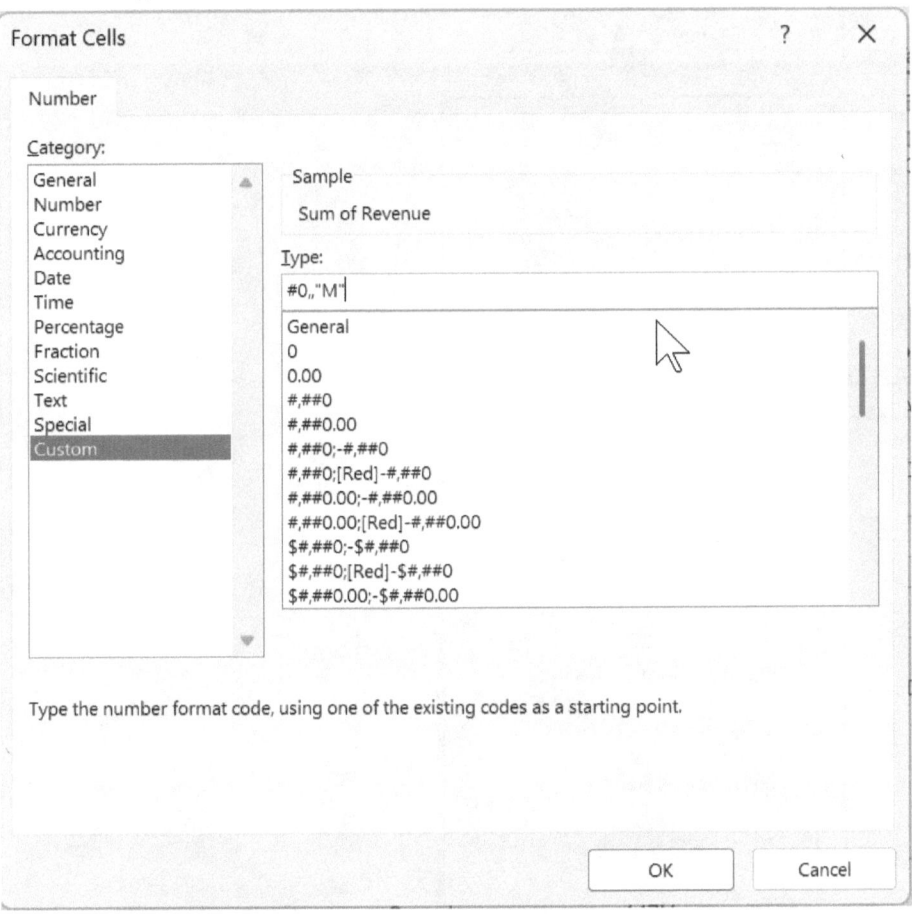

7. Right-click the PivotTable and click on **PivotTable Options**.

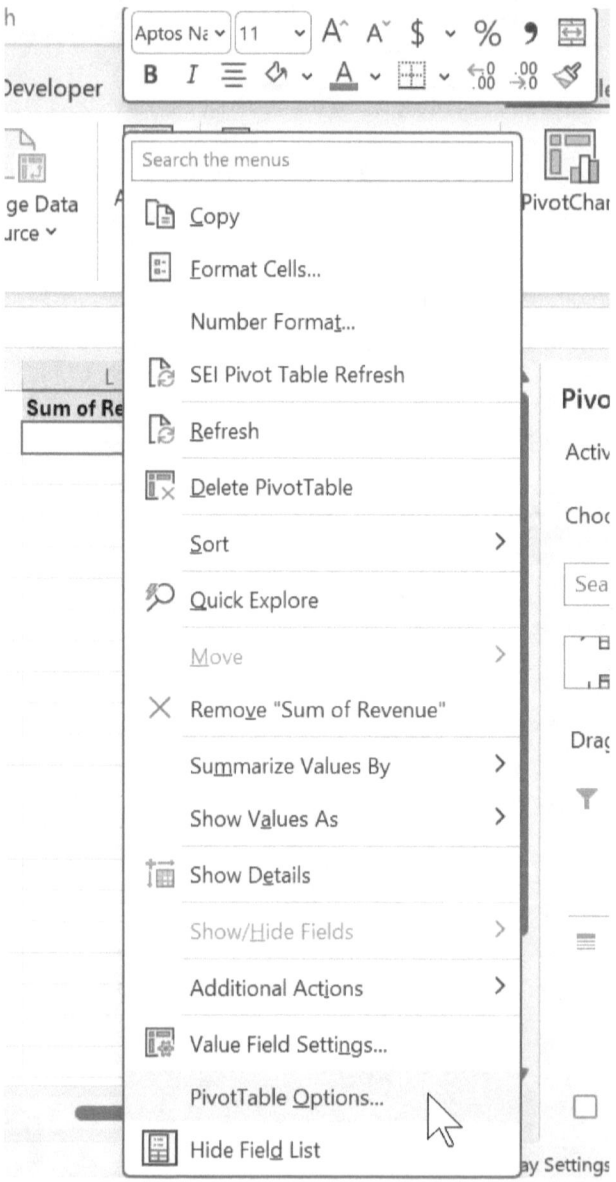

Creating (Power) Pivot Tables   113

8. Change the PivotTable Name field to **tRevenue**. Then, click **OK**.

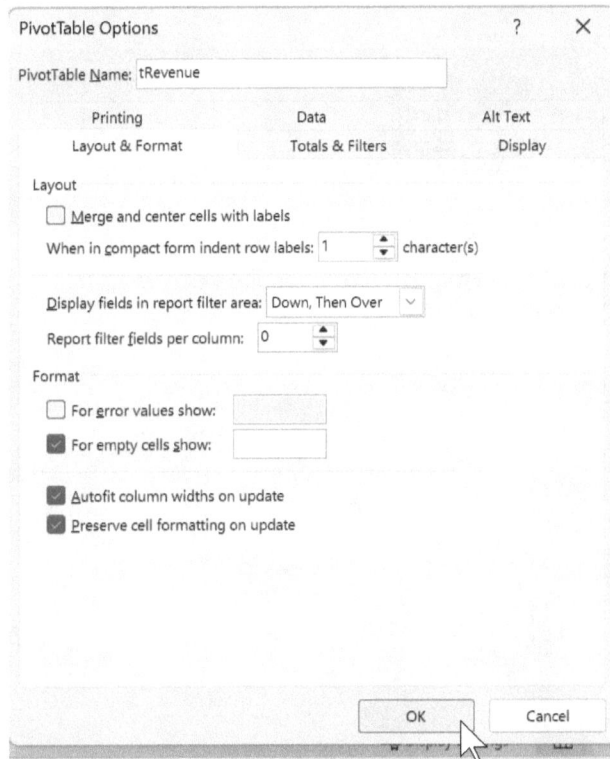

9. Select and copy the range **L1:L2** (the previous PivotTable). Then, paste on cell **N1**.

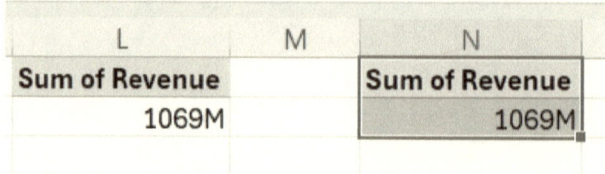

10. Add the field **Total Cost** and remove the **Sum of Revenue** in the **Value** section.

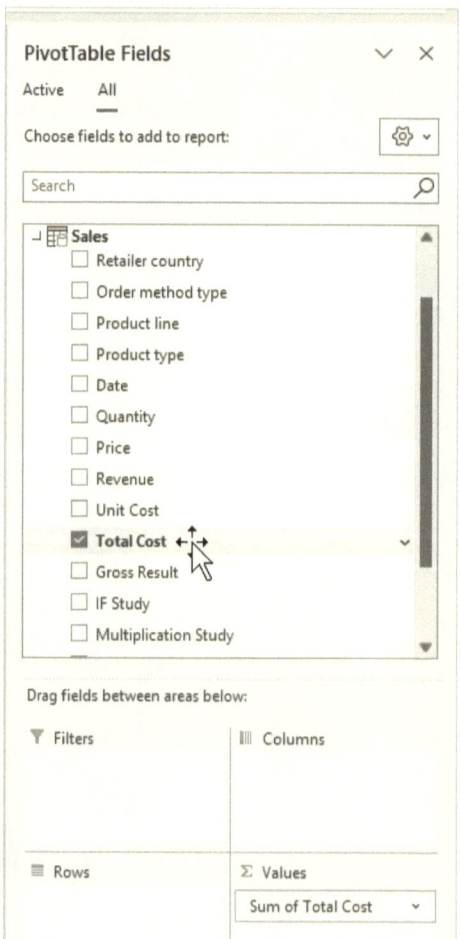

Creating (Power) Pivot Tables   115

11. In the **PivotTable Fields**, click **Sum of Total Cost** and select **Value Field Settings**.

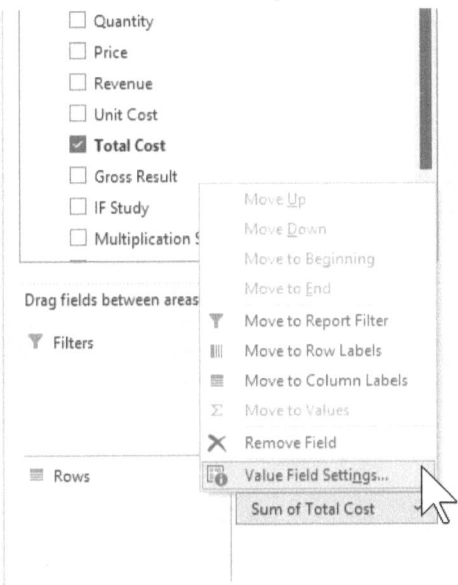

12. In the **Value Field Settings** window, click on **Number Format**.

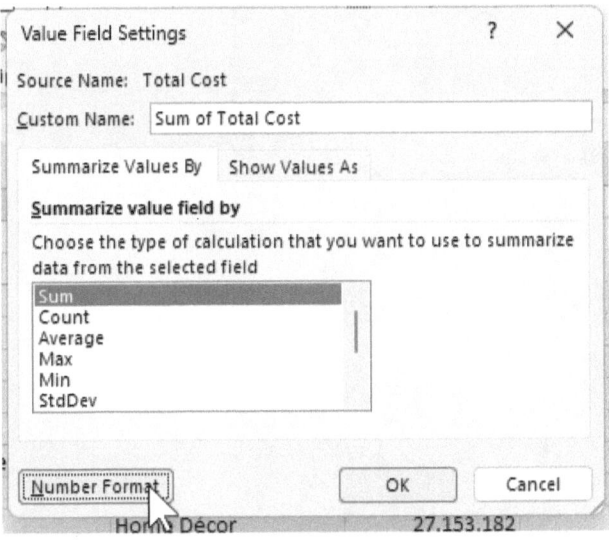

13. In the **Format Cells** window, go to **Number**, **Custom**, and type the format **#0,, "M"**. Then click **OK**.

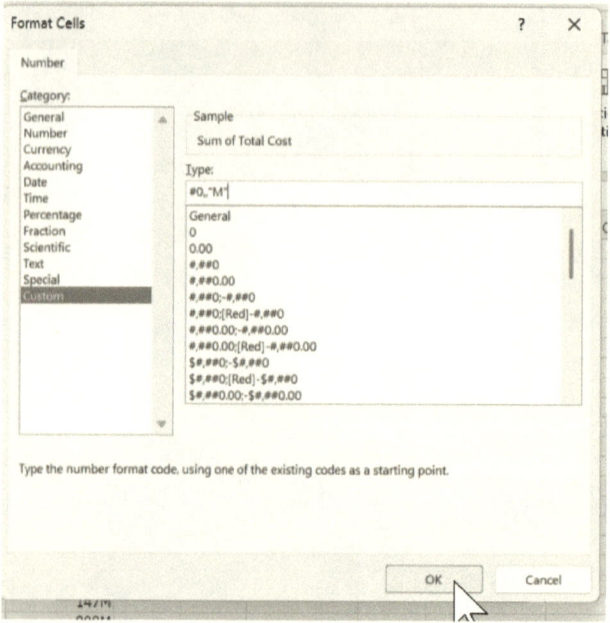

Creating (Power) Pivot Tables

14. Right-click the PivotTable and click on **PivotTable Options**.

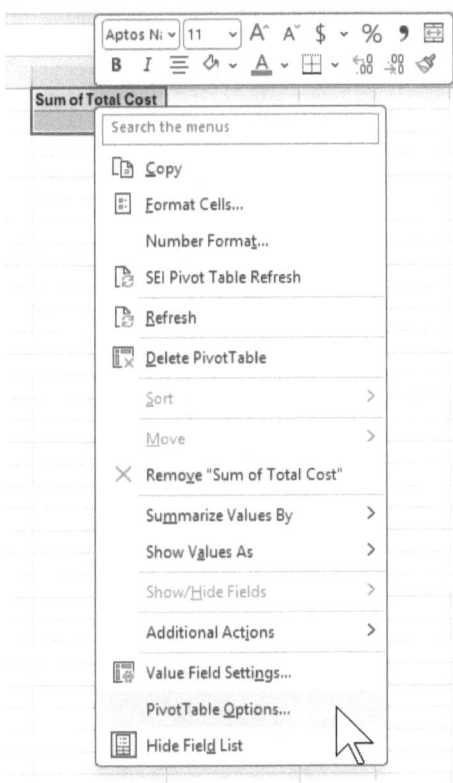

15. Change the **PivotTable Name** field to **tTotalCost**. Then, click **OK**.

Creating (Power) Pivot Tables

16. Select and copy the range **N1:N2**. Then, paste on cell **P1**.

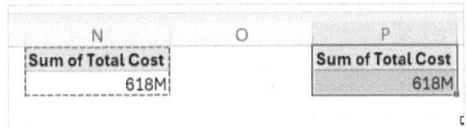

12. PivotTable Gross Margin

1. Add the measure **Gross Margin** and remove the field **Sum of Total Cost** in the **Value** section.

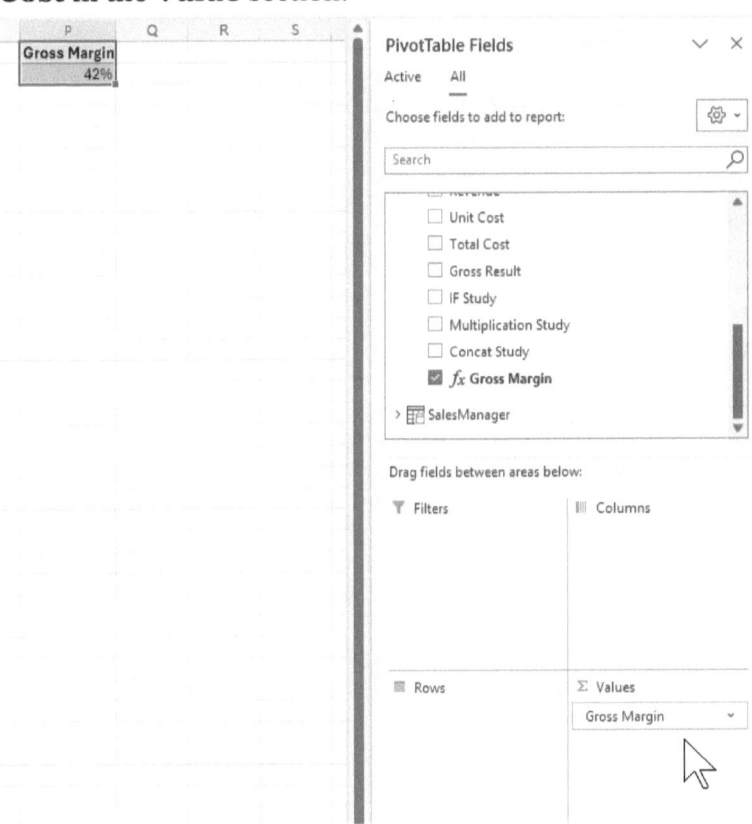

2. Right-click the PivotTable and click on **PivotTable Options**.

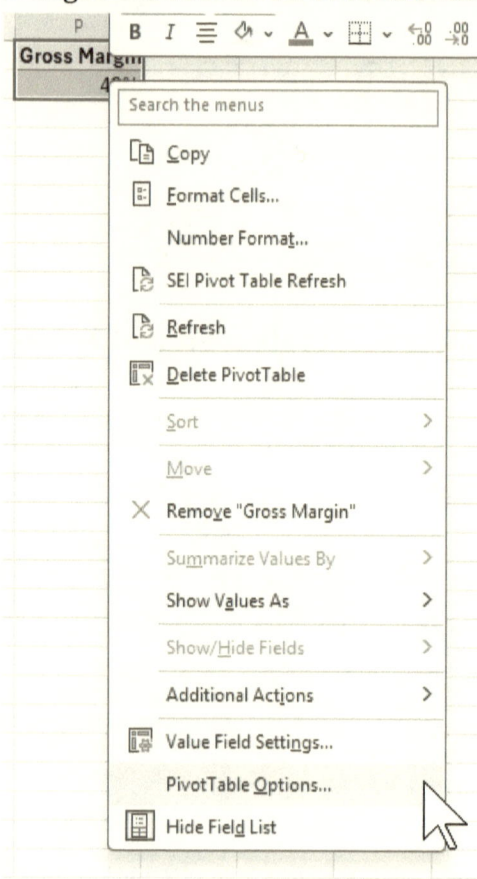

3. Change the **PivotTable name** to **tGrossMargin**. Then, click **OK**.

PivotTable Options		? ×
PivotTable Name: tGrossMargin		

Printing	Data	Alt Text
Layout & Format	Totals & Filters	Display

Layout
- ☐ Merge and center cells with labels
- When in compact form indent row labels: 1 character(s)

Display fields in report filter area: Down, Then Over
Report filter fields per column: 0

Format
- ☐ For error values show:
- ☑ For empty cells show:

- ☑ Autofit column widths on update
- ☑ Preserve cell formatting on update

[OK] [Cancel]

13. PivotTable Countries

1. Select cell **S1**, go to **Insert**, **PivotTable**, and select **From Data Model**.

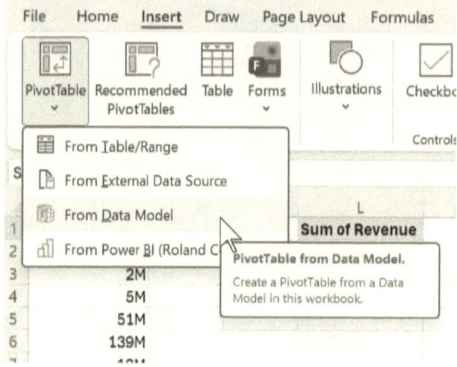

2. In the **PivotTable from Data Model** window, check the item **Existing Worksheet**. Then set the **Location** as **PivotTables!$S$1** and click **OK**.

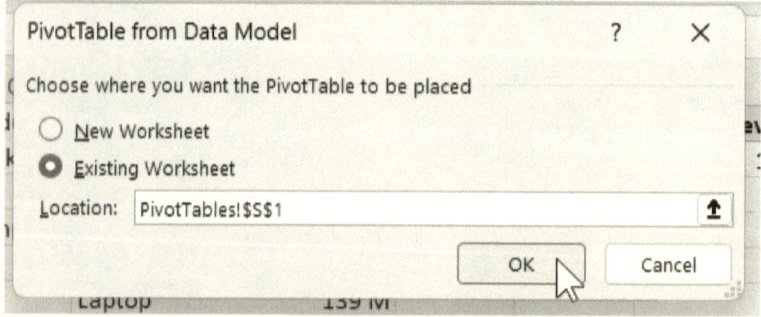

Creating (Power) Pivot Tables

3. If needed, right-click the PivotChart area and click on **Show Field List**.

4. Add the field **Country** in the **Rows** section and the field **Revenue** in the **Value** section

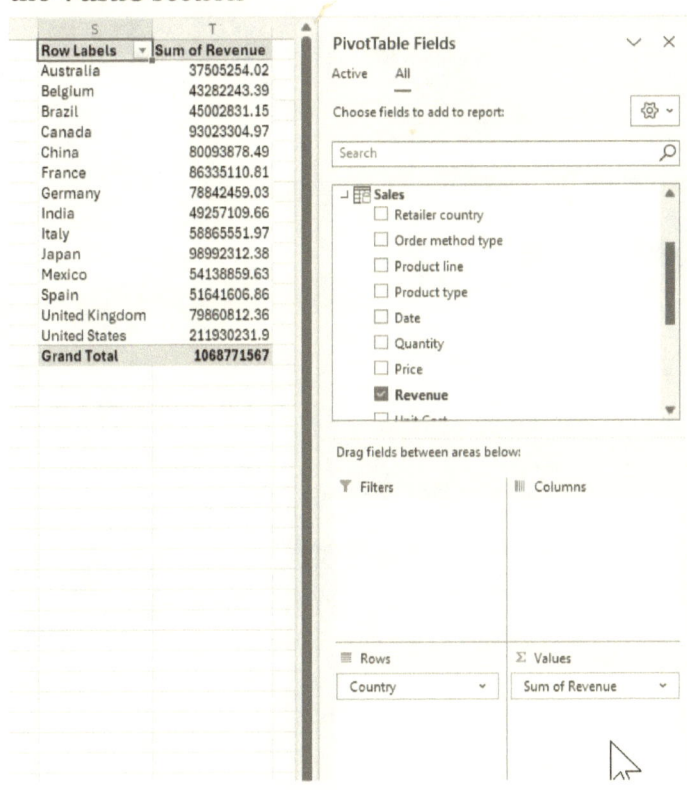

5. In the **PivotTable Fields,** click on **Sum of Revenue** and select **Value Field Settings**.

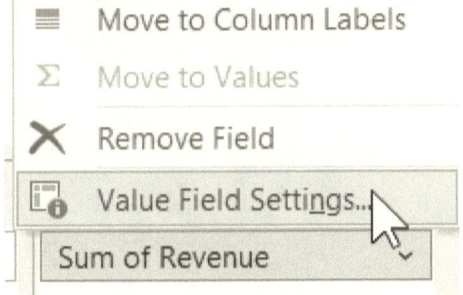

www.createandlearn.net

6. In the Value Field Settings window, click on Number Format.

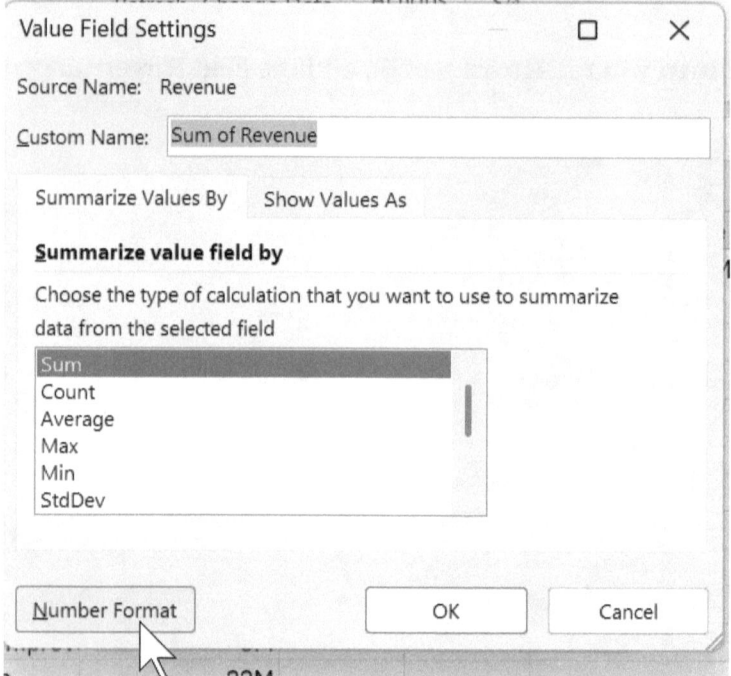

Creating (Power) Pivot Tables

7. In the **Format Cells** window, go to **Number**, **Custom**, and type the format **#0,, "M"**.

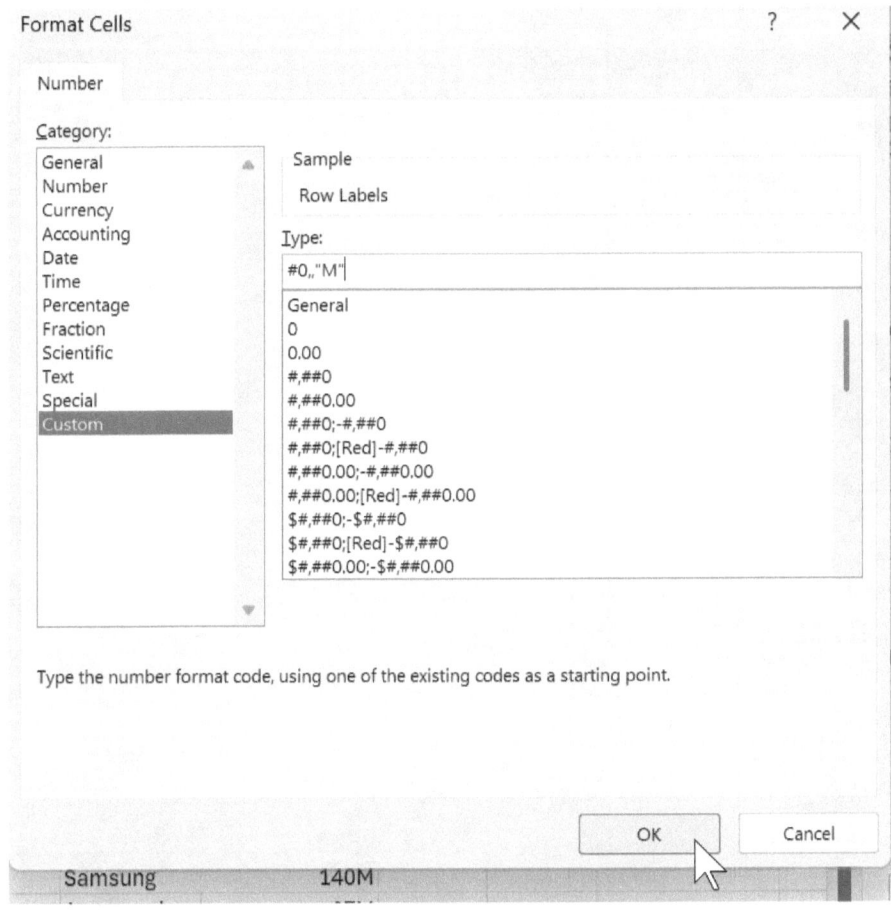

8. Right-click the PivotTable and click on **PivotTable Options**.

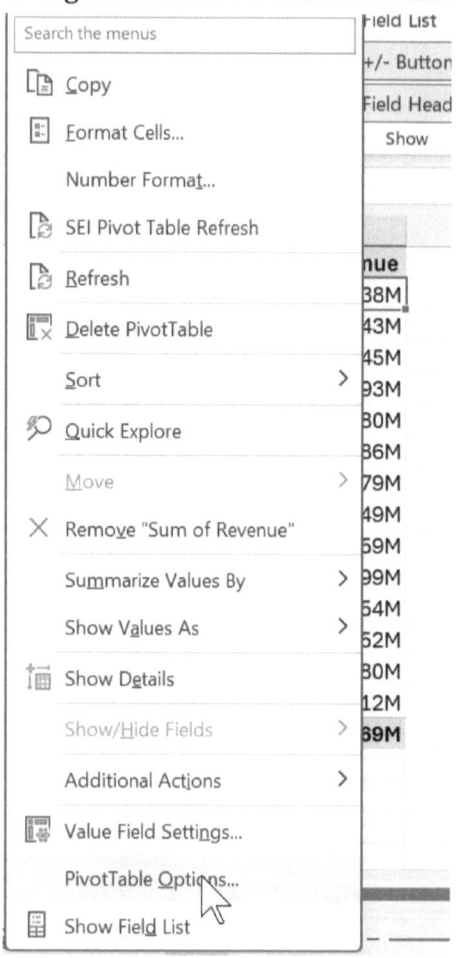

Creating (Power) Pivot Tables

9. Change the PivotTable Name to **tCountries**.

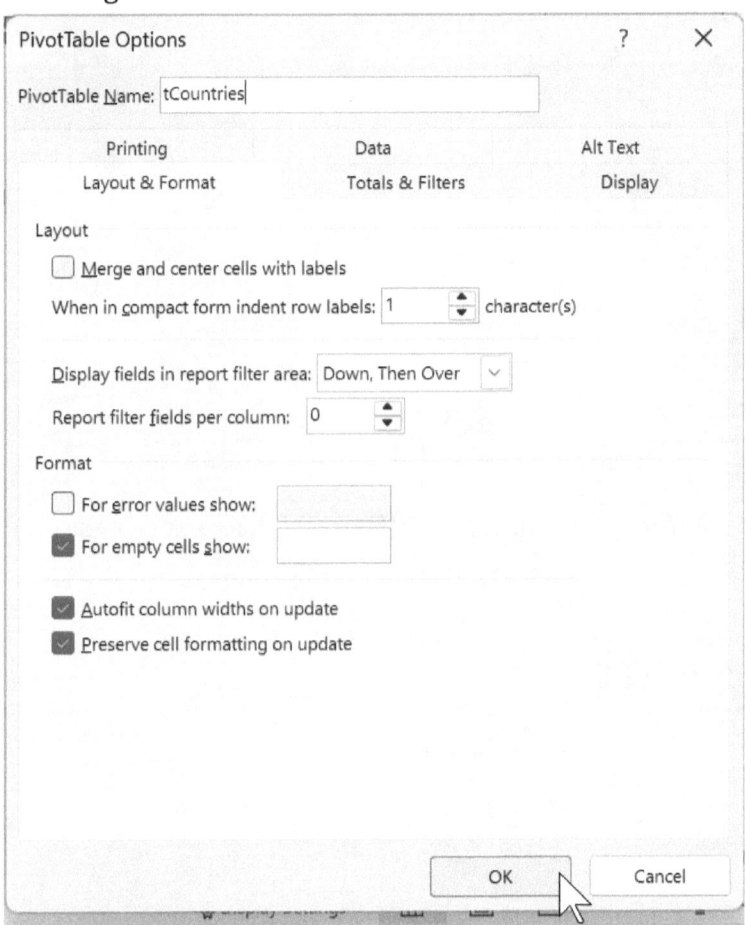

10. Go to the **Total & Filters** tab, and deselect the box **Show grand totals for Columnns**. Then, click **OK**.

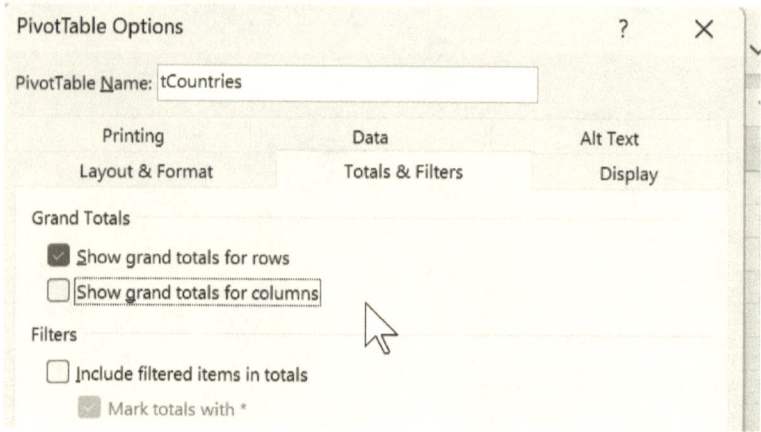

11. Select cell **V1** and type the formula **=IF(S1="","",S1)** and press **Enter**.

Creating (Power) Pivot Tables

12. Select cell **V1** and rest the cursor in the lower-right corner to turn it into a plus sign (+). Then, click and drag till cell **W1**. Then, do this again till cell **W15**. After you drop it, the formula will be copied to every cell in the range **V1:W15**.

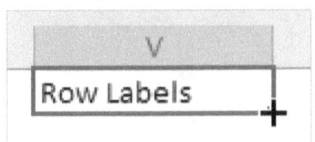

S	T	U	V	W
Row Labels	Sum of Revenue		Row Labels	Sum of Revenue
Australia	38M		Australia	37505254.02
Belgium	43M		Belgium	43282243.39
Brazil	45M		Brazil	45002831.15
Canada	93M		Canada	93023304.97
China	80M		China	80093878.49
France	86M		France	86335110.81
Germany	79M		Germany	78842459.03
India	49M		India	49257109.66
Italy	59M		Italy	58865551.97
Japan	99M		Japan	98992312.38
Mexico	54M		Mexico	54138859.63
Spain	52M		Spain	51641606.86
United Kingdom	80M		United Kingdom	79860812.36
United States	212M		United States	211930231.9

13. Select range **W2:W15**. Then, right-click the selection and click on **Format Cells**.

Creating (Power) Pivot Tables

14. In the **Format Cells** window, go to **Number**, **Custom**, and type the format **#0,, "M"**. Then click **OK**.

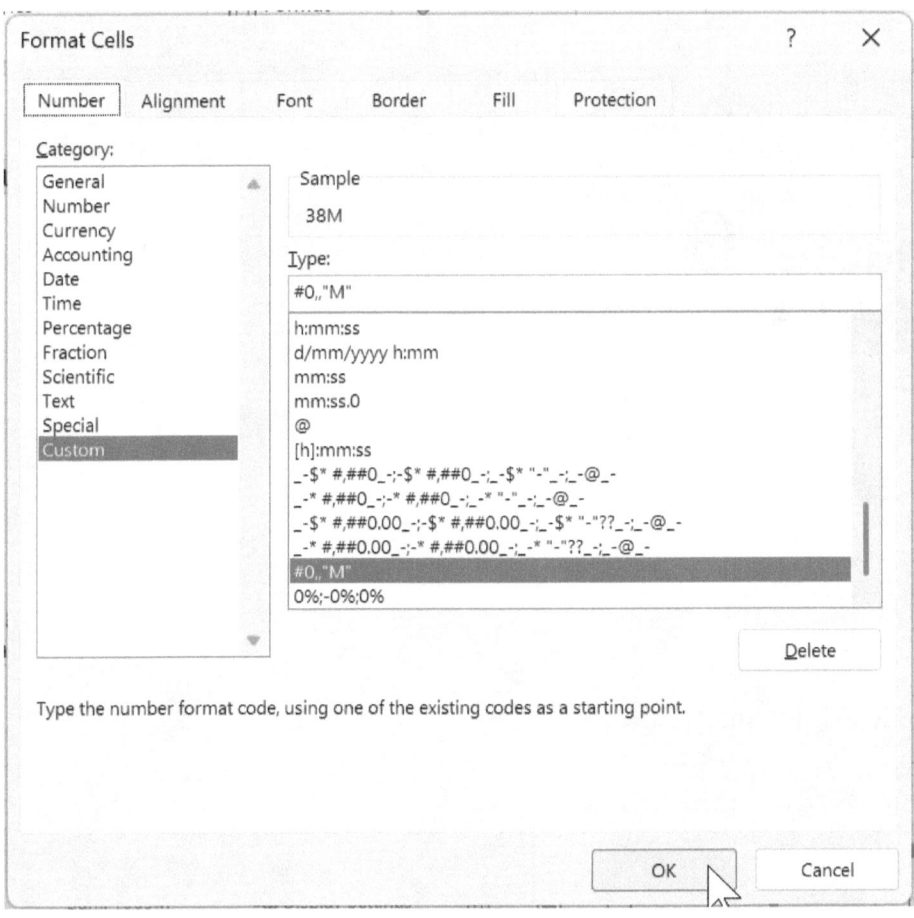

Chapter 6
Linking Data

1. Go to the Sales Dashboard tab.

2. Go to cell **F2** and type =

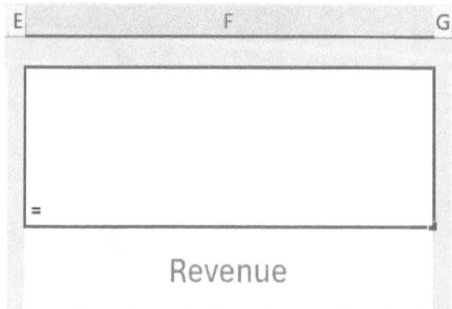

Linking Data

3. To link the data, go to the **PivotTables** tab and click on cell **L2**. Then press **Enter**. Excel will automatically create a GETPIVOTDATA formula/link.

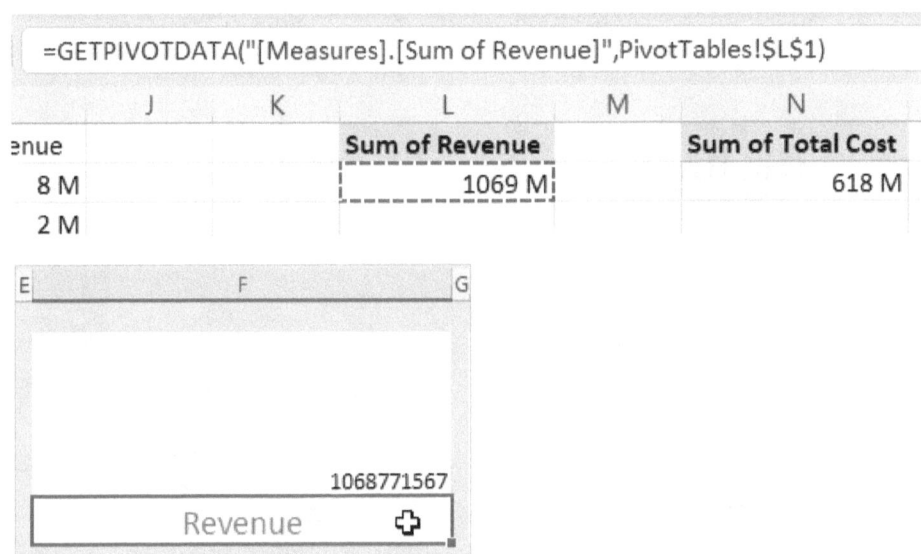

4. Go to cell **H2** and type =

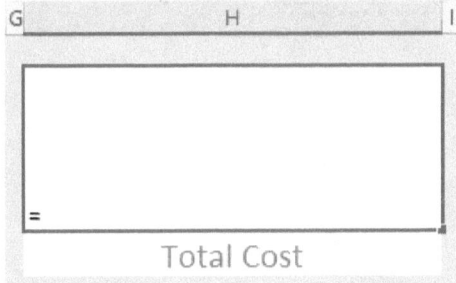

5. Go to the **PivotTables** tab and click on cell **N2**. Then press **Enter**.

I	J	K	L	M	N
=GETPIVOTDATA("[Measures].[Sum of Total Cost]",PivotTables!$N$1)					
Revenue			Sum of Revenue		Sum of Total Cost
8 M			1069 M		618 M
2 M					

6. Go to cell **J2** and type =

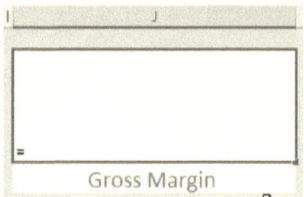

7. Go to the **PivotTables** tab and click on cell **P2**. Then press **Enter**.

N	O	P	Q
=GETPIVOTDATA("[Measures].[Gross Margin]",PivotTables!$P$1)			
Sum of Total Cost		Gross Margin	
618 M		42%	

Linking Data

8. The linked data in the **Sales Dashboard** tab should be like the image below.
9. Hold **CTRL** key and click on cells **F2**, **H2**, and **J2** to select them.

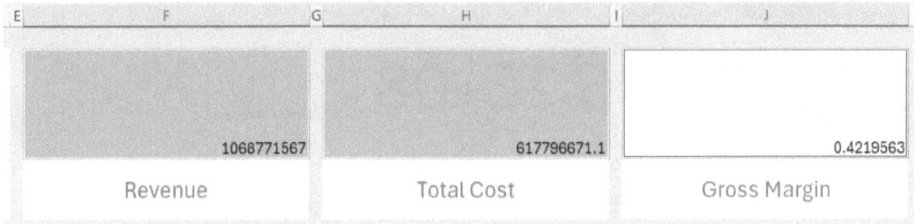

10. Go to the **Home** tab and change the **Font Size** to **48** and **Center** alignment.

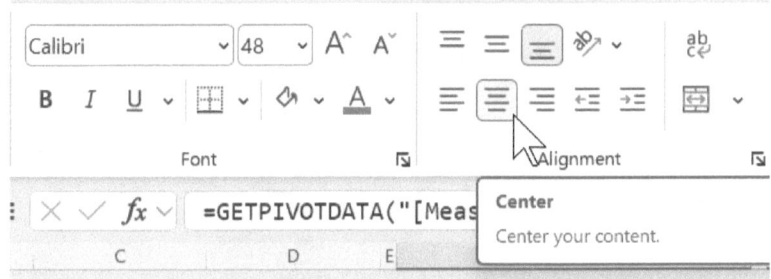

11. Hold the **CTRL** key and click on cells **F2** and **H2** to select them. Then right-click the selection and click on **Format Cells**.

13. In the **Format Cells** window, go to **Number, Custom**, and type the format **#0,, "M"**. Then click **OK**.

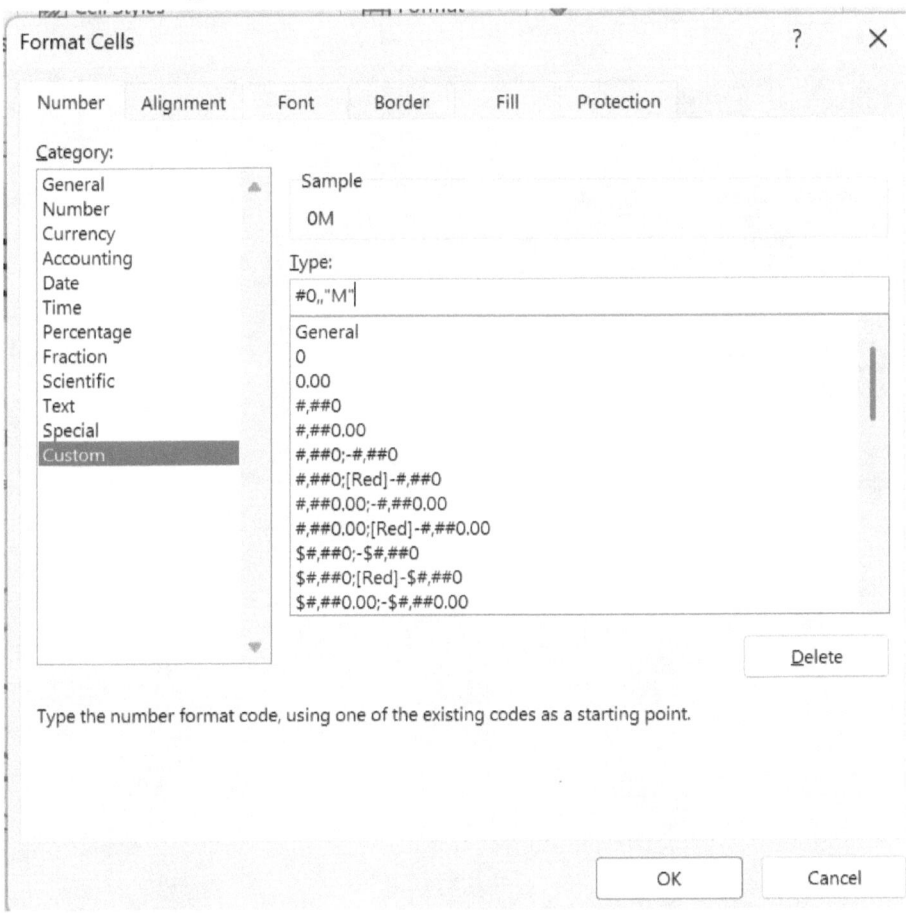

14. Select cell **J2** and click on **Percent Style**.

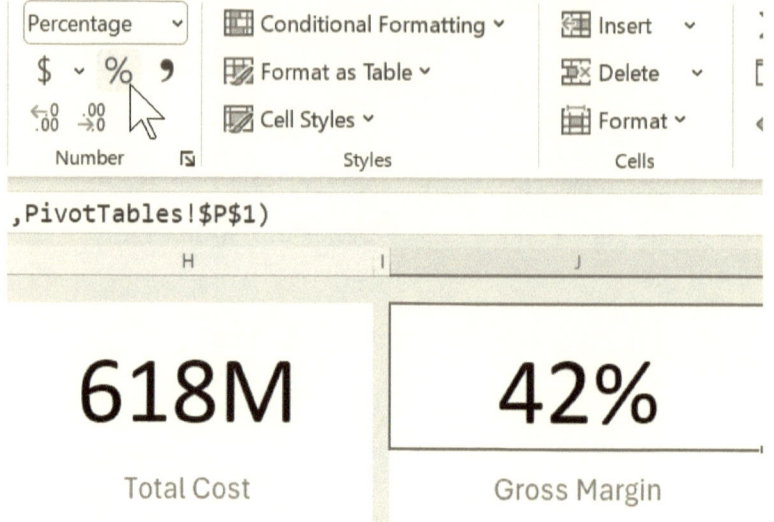

Linking Data

15. The Dashboard should be similar to the image below, so move objects and change formatting if necessary.

Chapter 7
Creating Special Visuals

14. Treemap

1. Go to the **PivotTables** tab and select the range **G1:I20**.

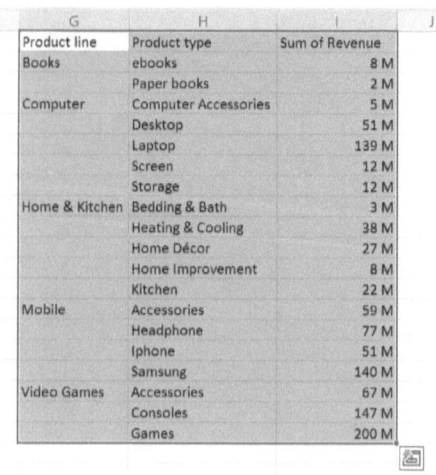

Creating Special Visuals

2. Go to the **Insert** tab and click on **Treemap**.

* If your Excel version does not have the Treemap chart, you can use different charts such as **Sunburst** or **Clustered Bar**.

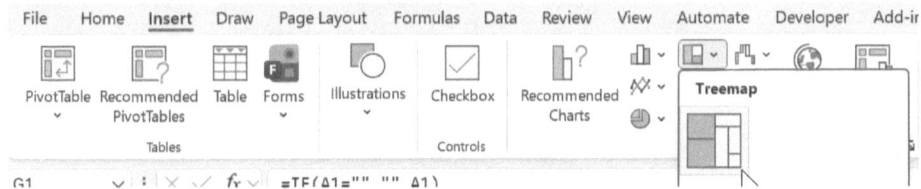

3. Change the Chart Title to **Revenue by Product Type**.

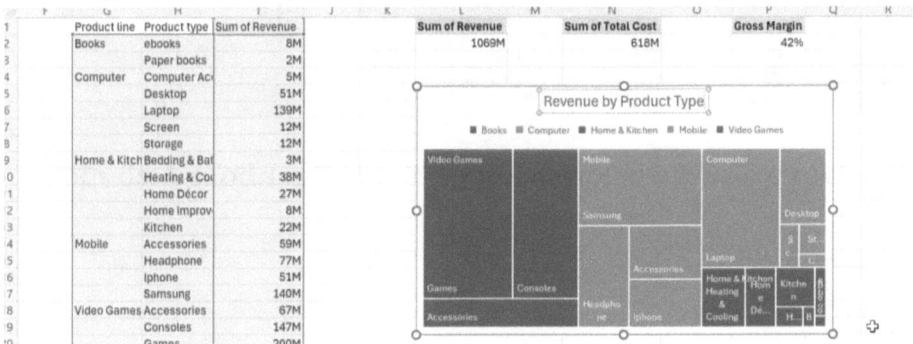

4. Right-click the chart area and click on **Move Chart**.

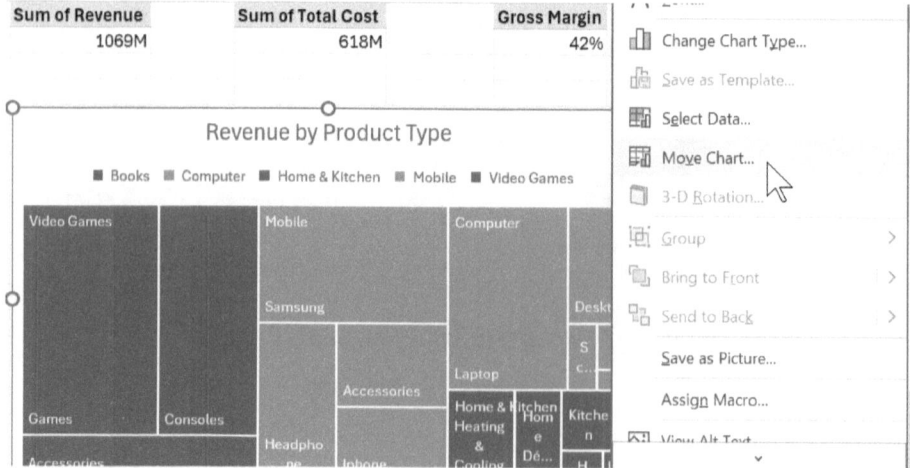

5. In the **Move Chart** window, select the **Sales Dashboard** tab and click **OK**.

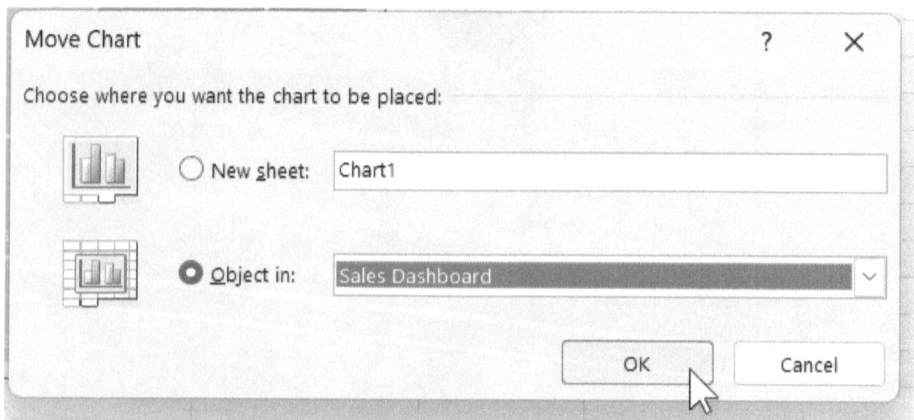

Creating Special Visuals

6. Go to the **Format** tab, **Shape Outline**, and click **No Outline**.

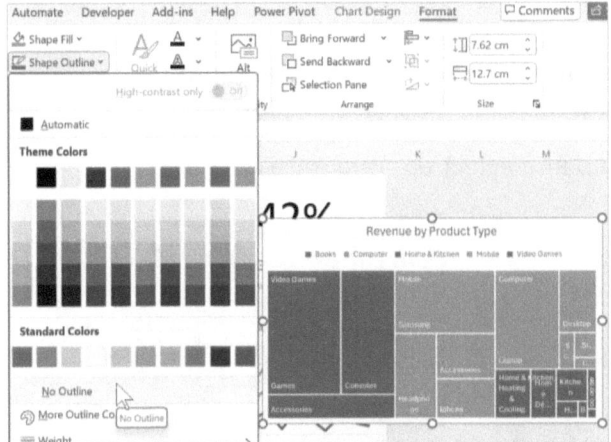

7. Drag and drop the chart to have a Dashboard like the image below.

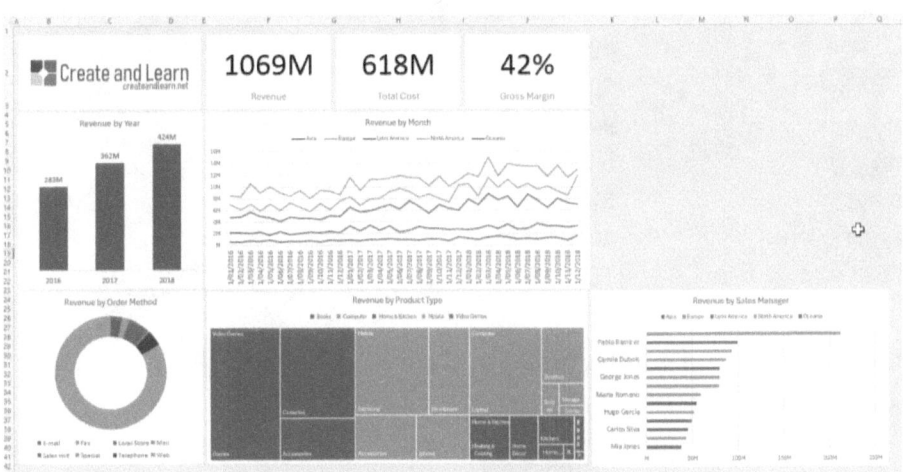

15. Field Map

Maps may require sign-in + internet. If countries don't render, clean/trim country names and confirm they are recognized.

1. Go to the **PivotTables** tab and select the range **V1:W15**.

S	T	U	V	W
Row Labels	Sum of Revenue		Row Labels	Sum of Revenue
Australia	38M		Australia	38M
Belgium	43M		Belgium	43M
Brazil	45M		Brazil	45M
Canada	93M		Canada	93M
China	80M		China	80M
France	86M		France	86M
Germany	79M		Germany	79M
India	49M		India	49M
Italy	59M		Italy	59M
Japan	99M		Japan	99M
Mexico	54M		Mexico	54M
Spain	52M		Spain	52M
United Kingdom	80M		United Kingdom	80M
United States	212M		United States	212M

2. Go to **Insert** tab, **Charts**, Maps, and click on **Filled Map**.

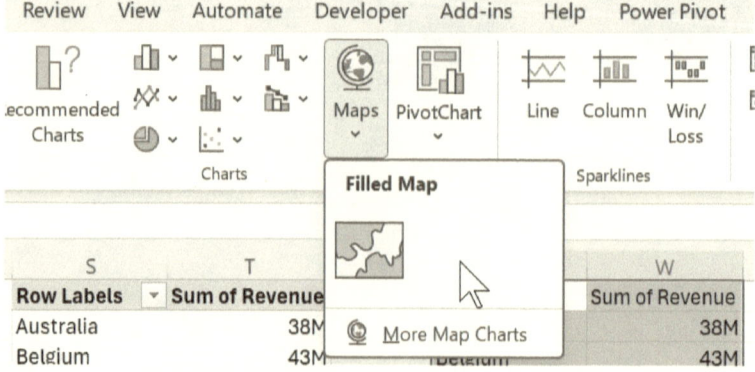

Creating Special Visuals

3. A new map will be created.

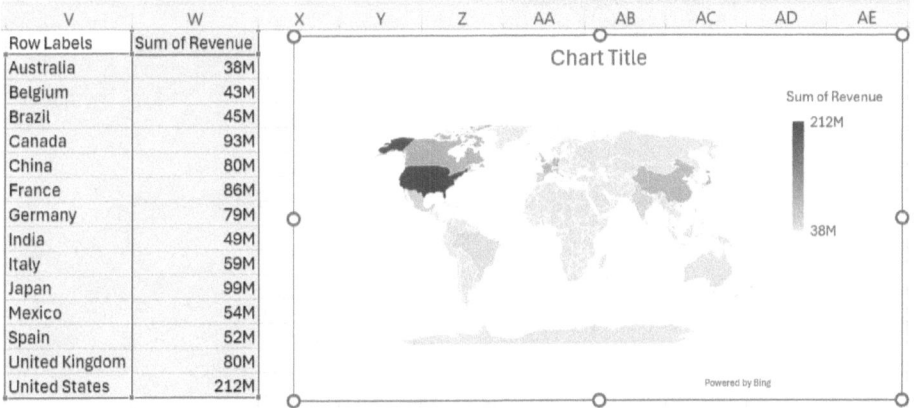

4. Select the map, go to the **Chart Design** tab, **Chart Styles**, and select **style 2**.

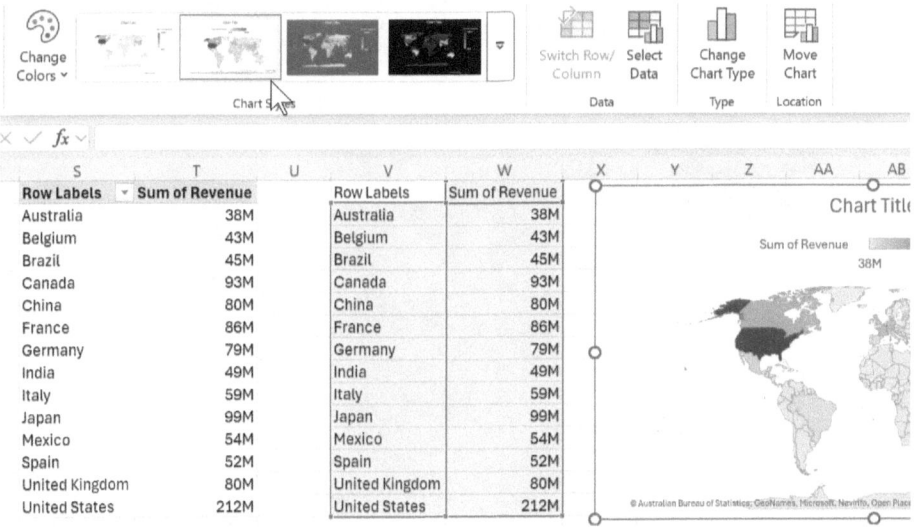

5. Go to **Chart Elements**, **Legend**, and select **Right**.

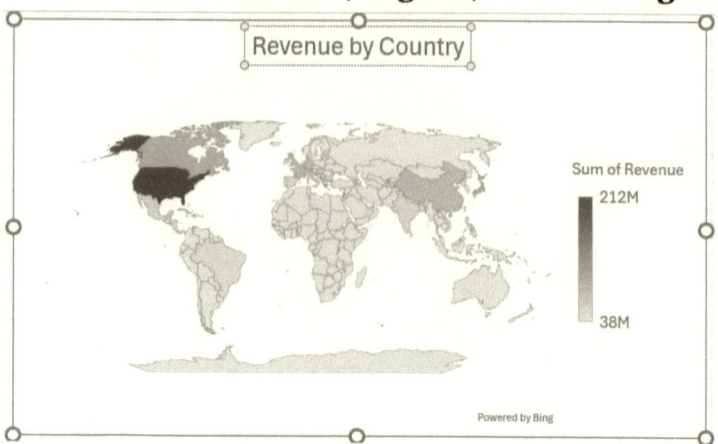

6. Double-click the **Chart Title** and type **Revenue by Country**.

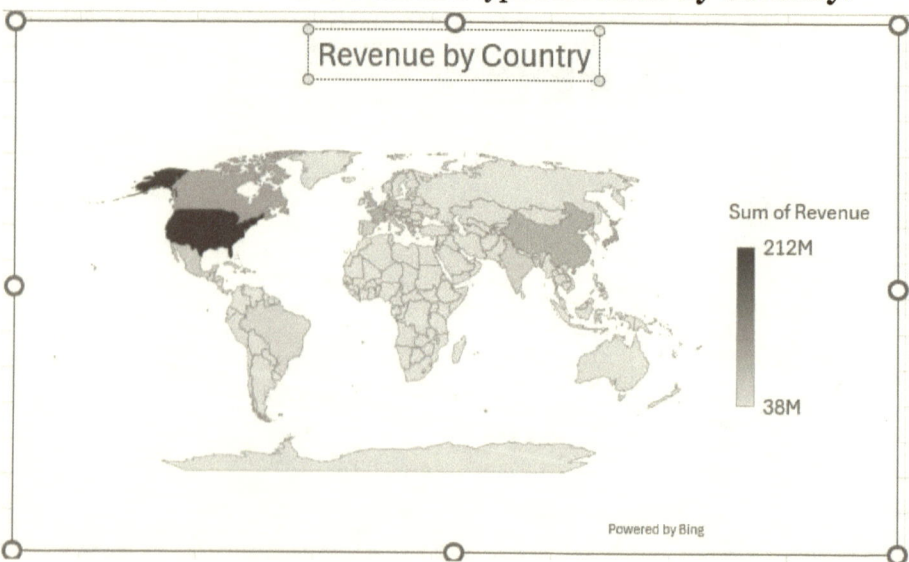

Creating Special Visuals

7. Right-click the **Chart Area** and click on **Move Chart**.

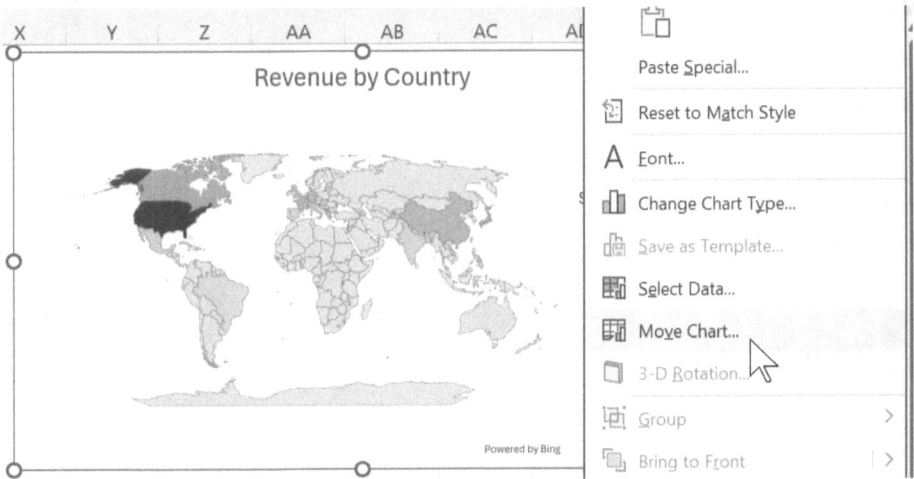

8. Check the option **Object in**, select **Sales Dashboard**, and click **OK**.

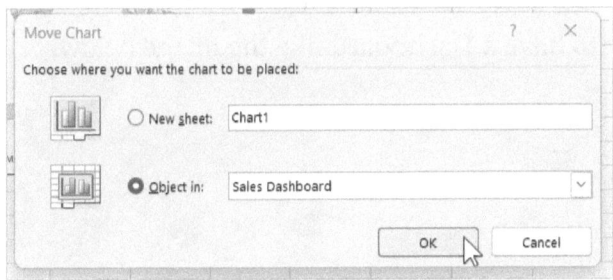

9. Select the map, go to the **Format** tab, **Shape Outline**, and click **No Outline**.

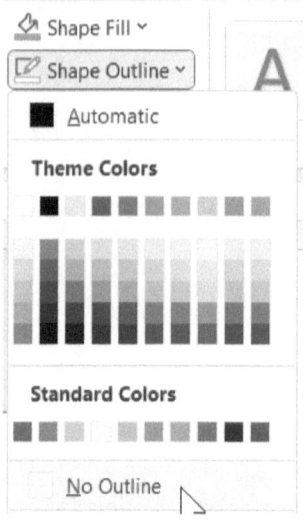

10. Drag and drop the chart to have a Dashboard like the image below.

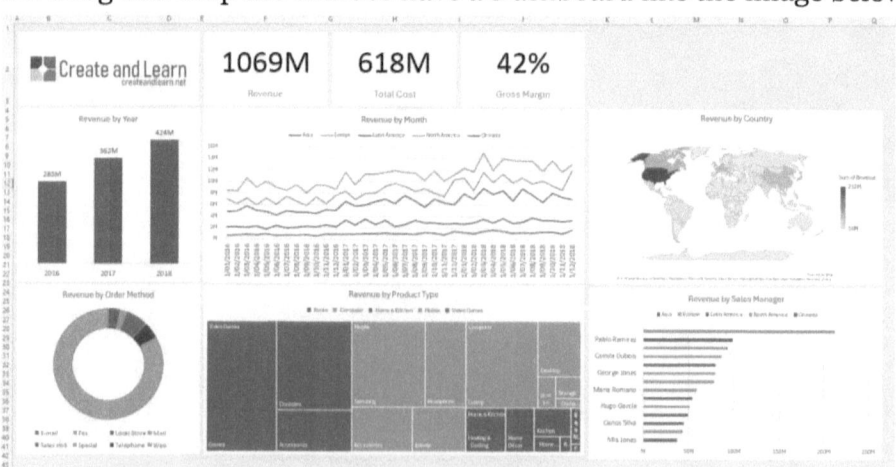

Slicer and Timeline

Chapter 8
Slicer and Timeline

The Slicer and Timeline are graphical selectors used to filter the data, and they can have different formats and point to other datasets.

Before continuing, let's change the workbook theme colors. Go to **Page Layout**, **Themes**, **Colors**, and select **Office 2013 – 2022**.

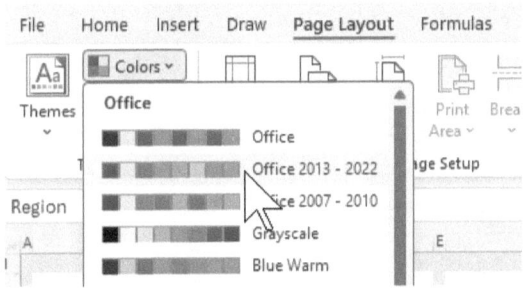

1. In the Sales Dashboard tab, go to the **Insert** tab and click on **Timeline**.

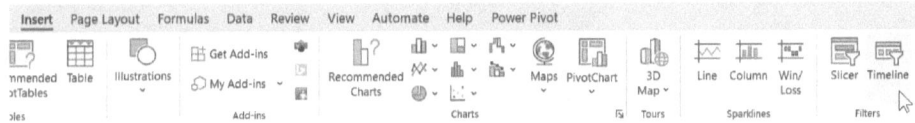

2. In the **Existing Connections** window, go to the **Data Model** tab, and select the **Tables in Workbook Data Model** option. Then, click **Open**.

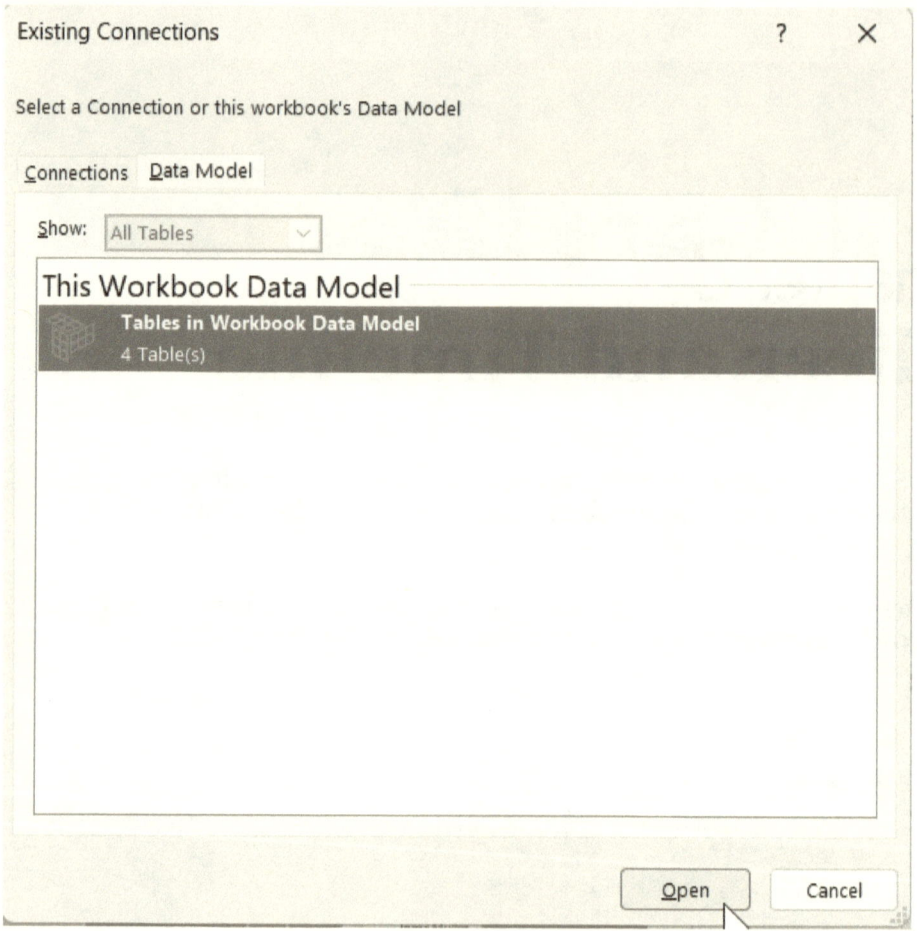

Slicer and Timeline

3. In the **Insert Timelines** window, go to the **All** tab and select the field **date** in the **Sales** table. Then click **OK**.

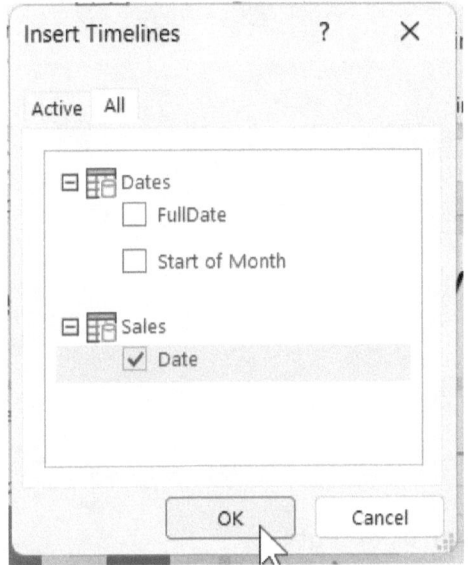

4. In the new timeline, change the display period to **YEARS**.

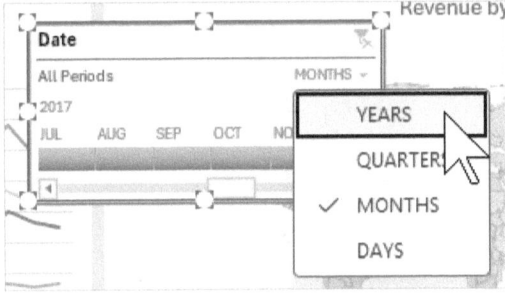

www.createandlearn.net

5. Right-click the timeline and click on **Report Connections**.

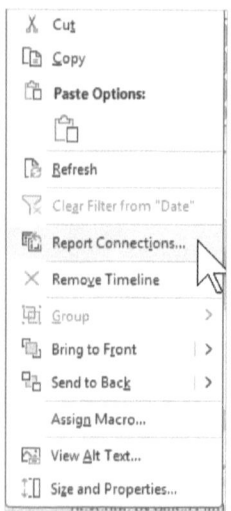

6. Check all the PivotTables and PivotCharts, except for **cRevenueByYear**. Then click **OK**. The timeline filter will be applied to all visuals but the last chart (the Revenue by Year needs to show all years even if a date filter is changed).

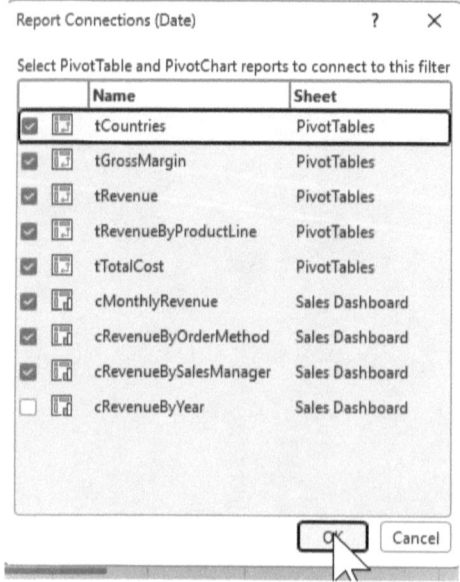

Slicer and Timeline

7. Go to the **Insert** tab and click on **Slicer**.

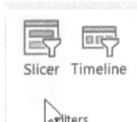

In the **Existing Connections** window, go to the **Data Model** tab and select the **Tables in Workbook Data Model** option. Then, click **Open**.

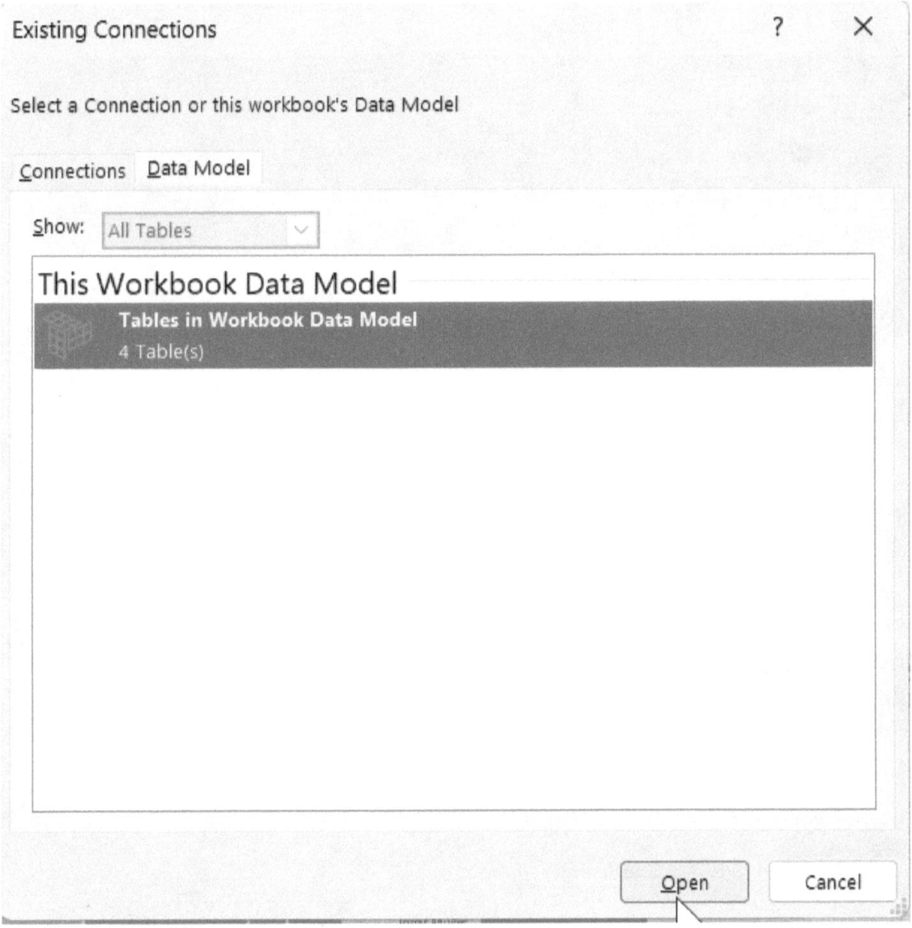

8. In the **Insert Slicers** window, go to the **All** tab and select the field **Region** in the Region table. Then click **OK**.

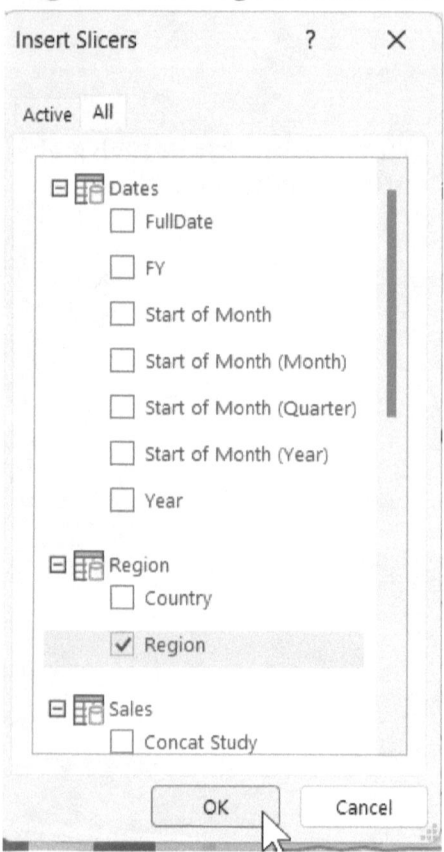

9. Move the slicer close to the timeline filter.

10. Go to the **Insert** tab and click on **Slicer**.

11. In the **Existing Connections** window, go to the **Data Model** tab and select the **Tables in Workbook Data Model** option. Then, click **Open**.

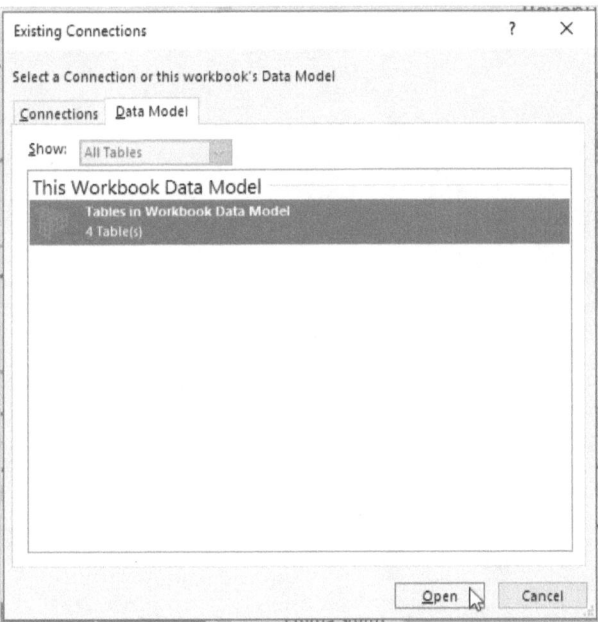

12. In the **Insert Slicers** window, go to the **All** tab and select the field **Product line** in the Sales table. Then click **OK**.

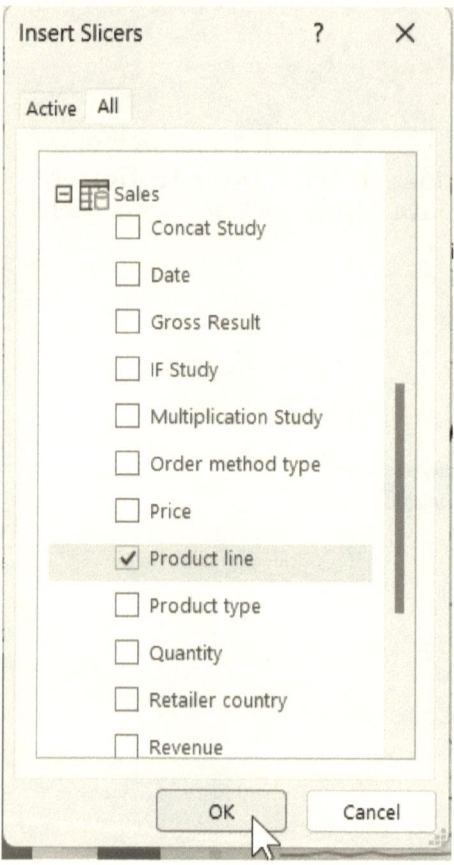

13. Select the **Region** slicer and go to **Slicer** tab and on **Slicer Styles** select the **Light Blue Style**. Repeat this step with both slicers.

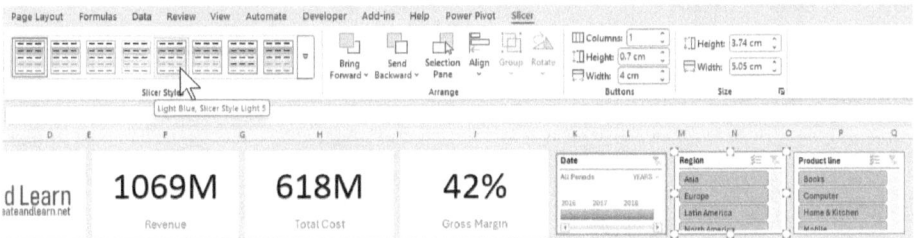

14. Select the timeline, go to the **Timeline** tab, and change the style.

15. Right-click the **Region** slicer and click on **Report Connections**.

Slicer and Timeline

16. Select all the PivotCharts and PivotTables and click **OK**. Repeat this step with the **Product Line** slicer.

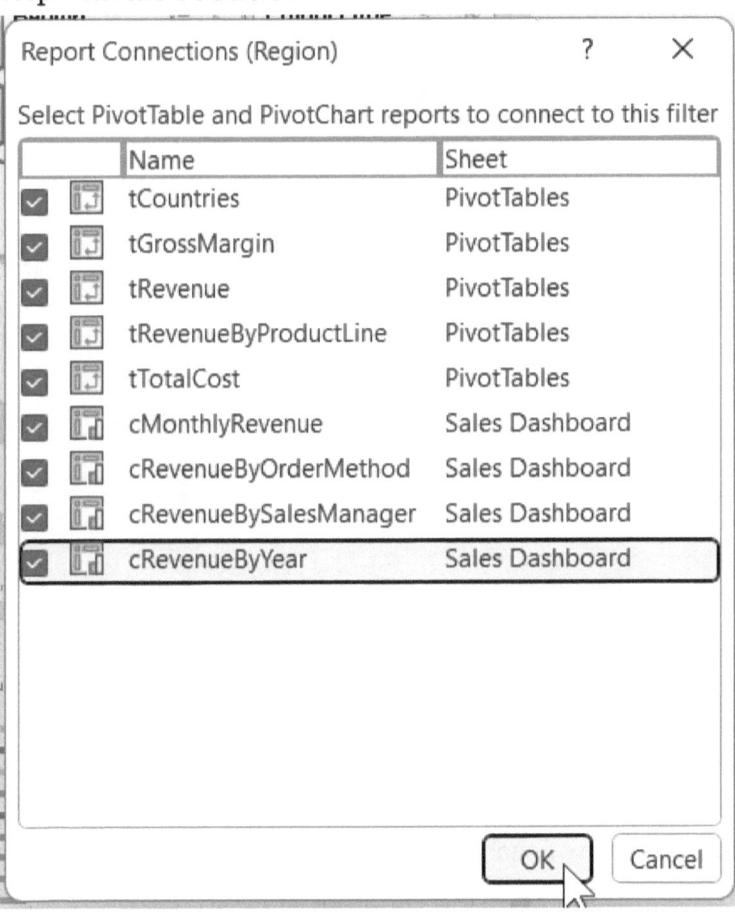

17. Click on Date **2017**, Region **Asia** and **Europe**, and Product line **Books**. Click on the **Multi-Select**, button to allow multiple items selection.

18. Play around with the filters and see how the charts behave. Note that the **Revenue by Year** chart will not be affected by the **Date** filter.

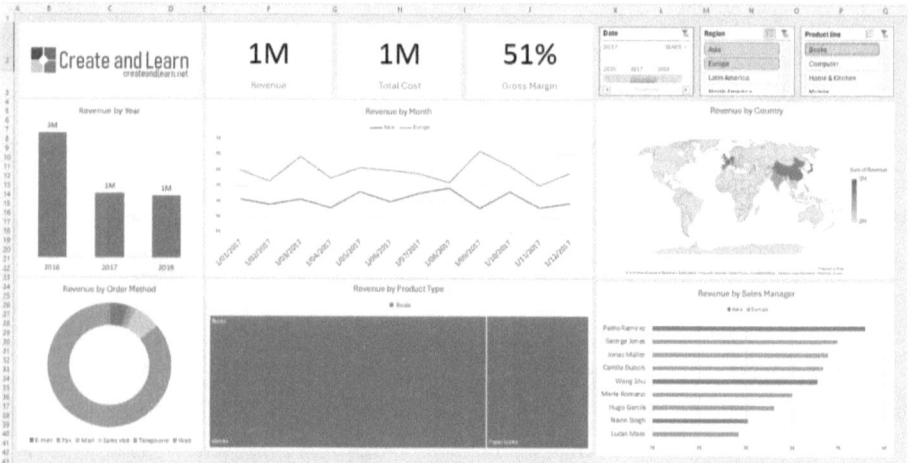

19. Click on the **Clear Filter** of each Slicer to restore the selection. And Select 2018,

www.createandlearn.net

Chapter 9
Setup Printing

1. Click on the bottom-right corner, **Page Break Preview**.

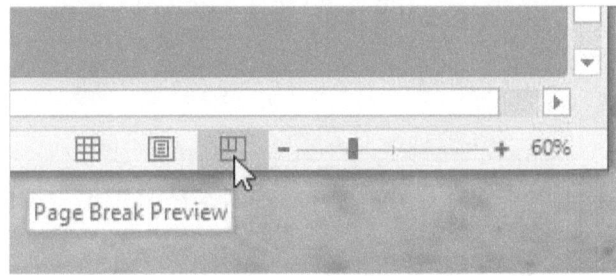

2. This view will show the page limits whenever you need to print the document.

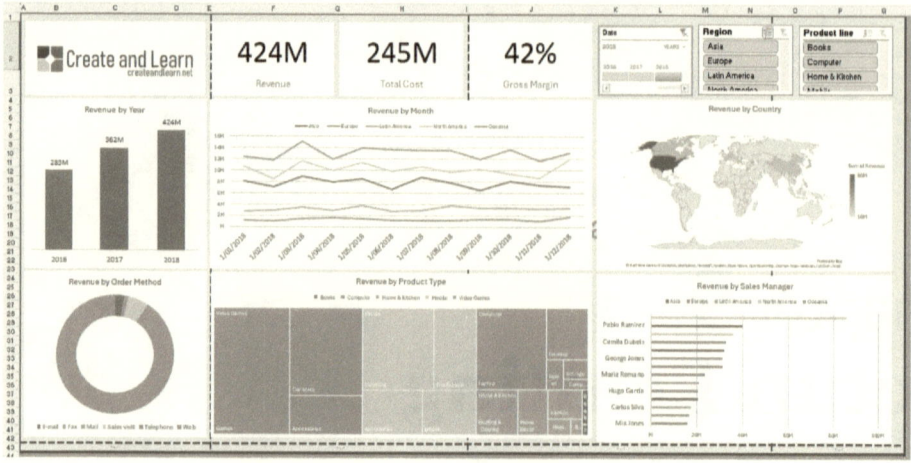

3. Go to the **Page Layout** tab and change the scale to **1 page** of width and **1 page** of height.

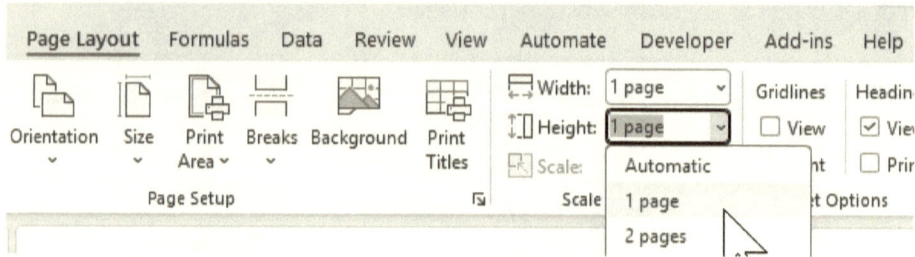

4. Change the Orientation to Landscape.

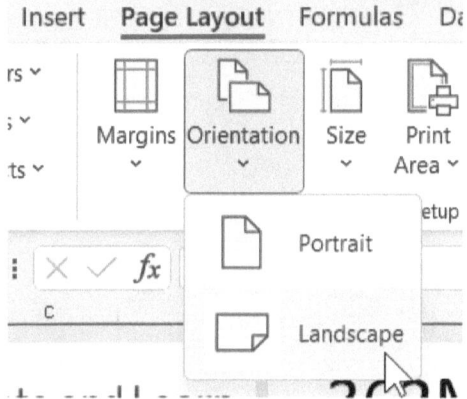

5. Click on **Margins** and change it to **Narrow**.

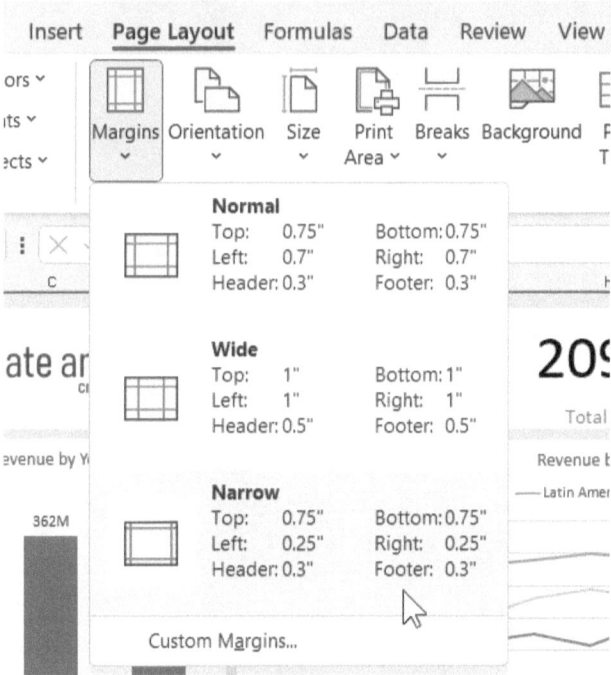

6. Click on the right-corner **Page Setup**.

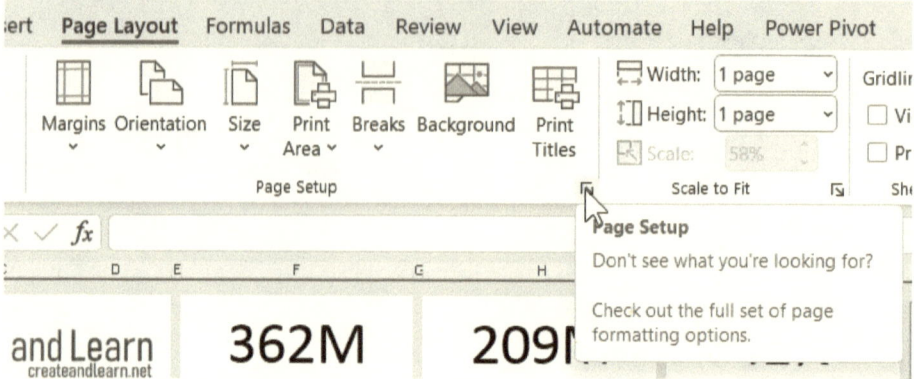

7. In the **Page Setup** window, go to the **Margins** tab and select the **Center on page** to **Horizontally** and **Vertically**. Then click **OK**.

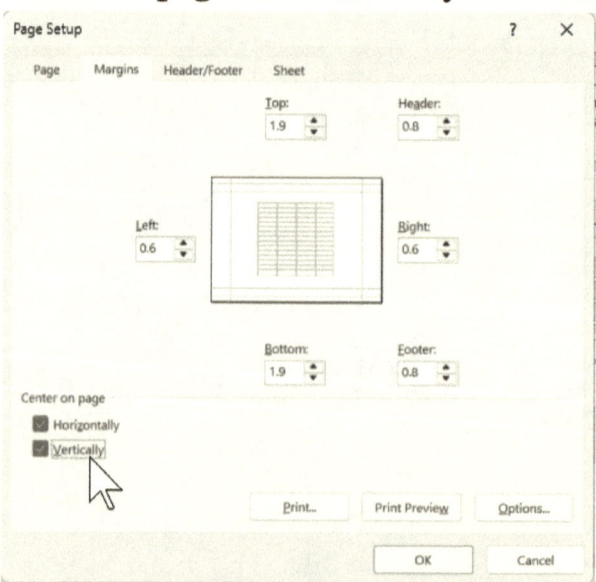

Setup Printing 165

8. Click on the **File** tab, **Print,** and check how the Dashboard will look if printed.

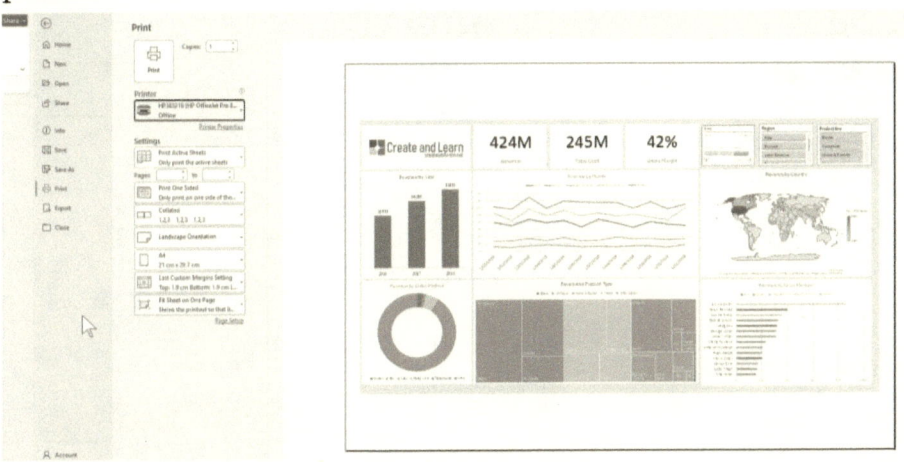

9. In the **File** tab, go to **Options**, **Advanced**, and deselect **Show page breaks**. Then click **OK**.

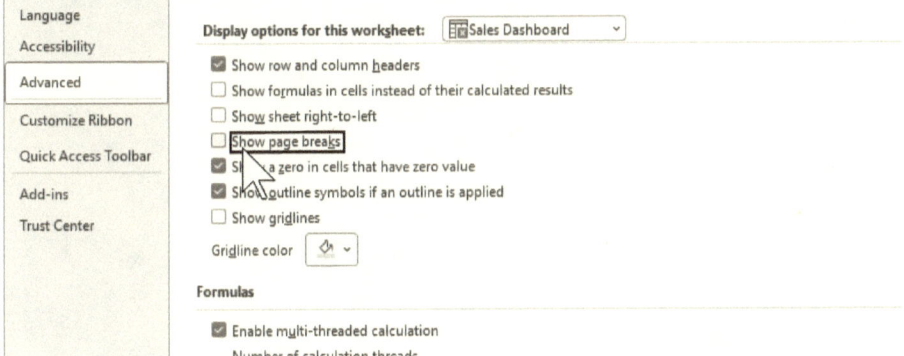

www.createandlearn.net

10. On the right corner, click on **Normal View**.

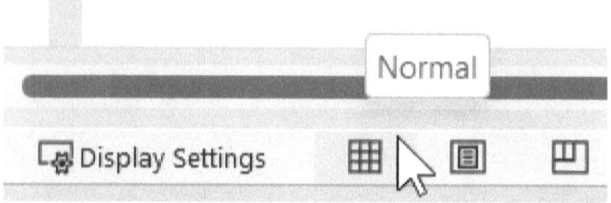

Chapter 10
Sharing online

You can share your file with other Excel users and let them view or edit the workbook.

1. Go to the right corner and click on **Share**.

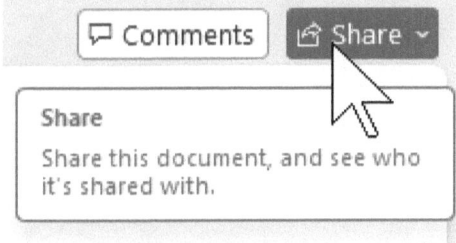

2. If you are not signed in to your OneDrive account, it will ask you to **sign in** or **create** one.

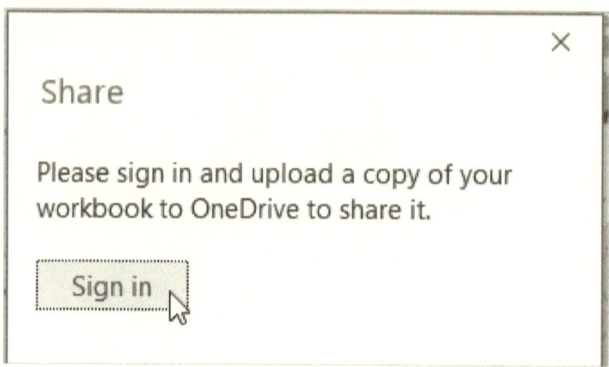

3. Once signed in, you can save the file online or attach it to an email. Click on Share through OneDrive. Excel will request a copy of your file saved on your OneDrive account.

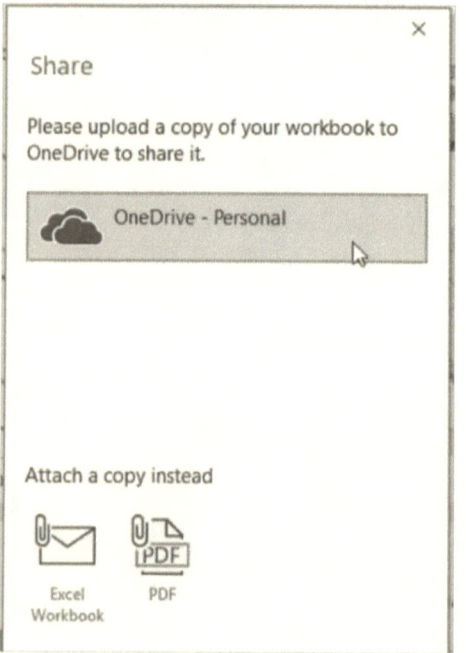

4. In the Share bar, type the email to be shared.

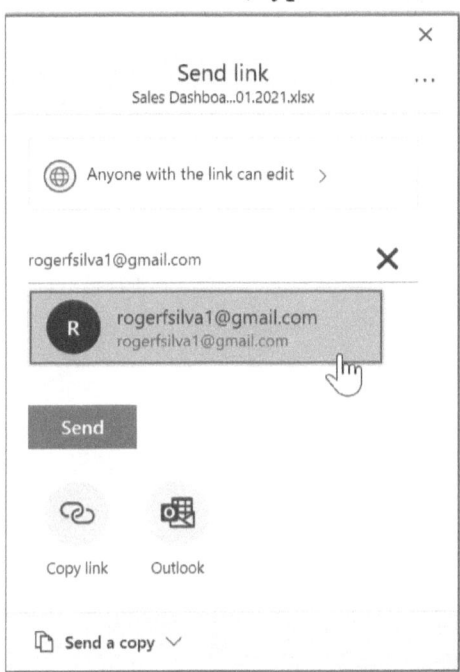

5. You also can change the option to **Allow editing**.

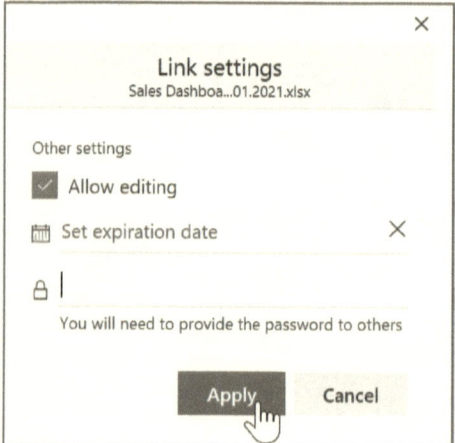

Sharing online   171

6. The person you have shared the file with will see it in the **OneDrive** account at the **Shared** session or the **Shared with me** in Excel.

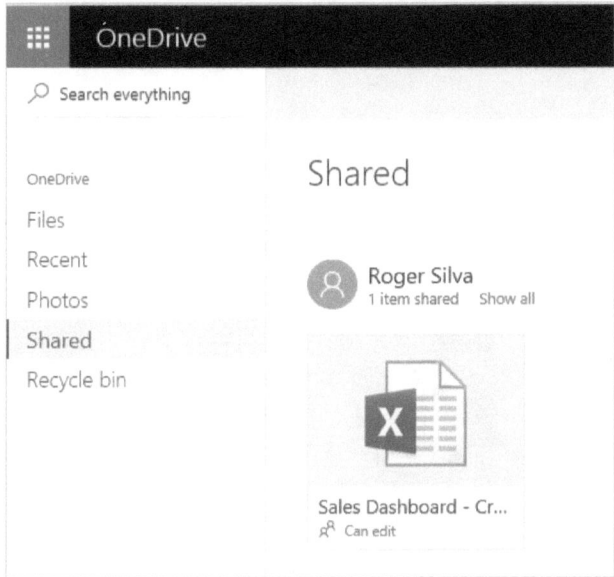

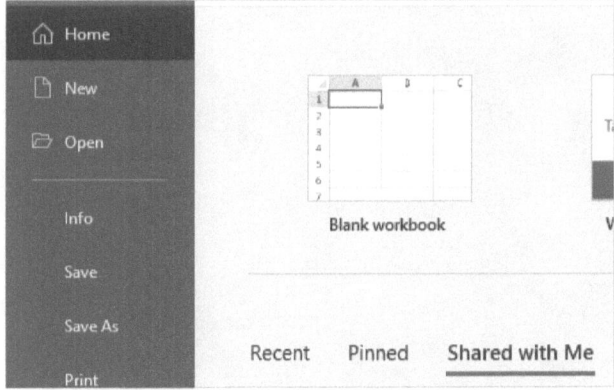

www.createandlearn.net

7. **Congratulations**! You have created a complete Dashboard using Power Query, Data Model, Power Pivot, and many other essential tools.

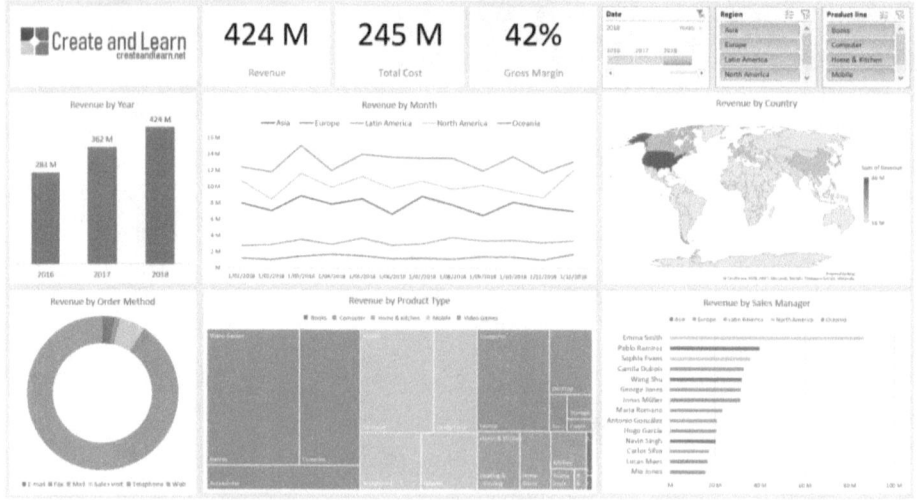

Next Steps

This book was created to help you learn by doing and through practice and expanding your knowledge in Excel and its Power Suite.
If you want to keep practicing and improving your knowledge through several industries, I have a few recommendations:

1- Modify the current dashboard. Try using other graphics, fonts, themes, and visuals.

2- Try to build the dashboard for this book without assistance. Refer to this book only when necessary.

3- Try the **Excel Easy** book series, where you can practice and learn from various industry metrics and datasets.

Visit the page createandlearn.net/exceleasy to have access to these books and more.

4- Spread the word. Share your dashboard with colleagues and on social media like LinkedIn. Add me to your network so I can comment and check your progress on LinkedIn. You will find me as Roger F. Silva.

5- Follow us on social media, search for Create and Learn, and find us on **YouTube**, **Instagram**, **Facebook**, and **LinkedIn**. We publish weekly material about business intelligence.

6- Do not stop! Learning has never been more accessible. Search websites, books, and videos, and don't stop studying. This is an excellent way to maintain a healthy brain and a promising career!

Final words

Thank you for the journey! I hope that you have enjoyed and learned from this book.

Although the Business Intelligence concept is not new, the tools and methods have changed dramatically in recent years, and you made the right decision to learn more about this.

Also, I would like to ask you to take a minute to **review** my book. A good rating and your positive feedback are incredibly **important** for my work. If you have any comments or suggestions, please email me or message me on LinkedIn — I will be more than happy to hear from you and have you on my network.

Again, take a minute to **review** my book on the website from which you bought it, and send me your **feedback** if you want.

Thank you for the time we spent creating and learning.

Roger F. Silva

Contact.createandlearn@gmail.com
createandlearn.net
www.linkedin.com/in/roger-f-silva

www.createandlearn.net

You can find more Create and Learn books, files, articles, and videos:

https://www.createandlearn.net/

https://www.amazon.com/Roger-F-Silva/e/B07JC8J1L5/

http://www.facebook.com/createandlearn.net

https://www.linkedin.com/company/create-and-learn

https://www.instagram.com/createandlearn_net/

https://www.youtube.com/c/createandlearn

www.createandlearn.net

Final words

For more **Create and Learn** books, visit
https://www.createandlearn.net/:

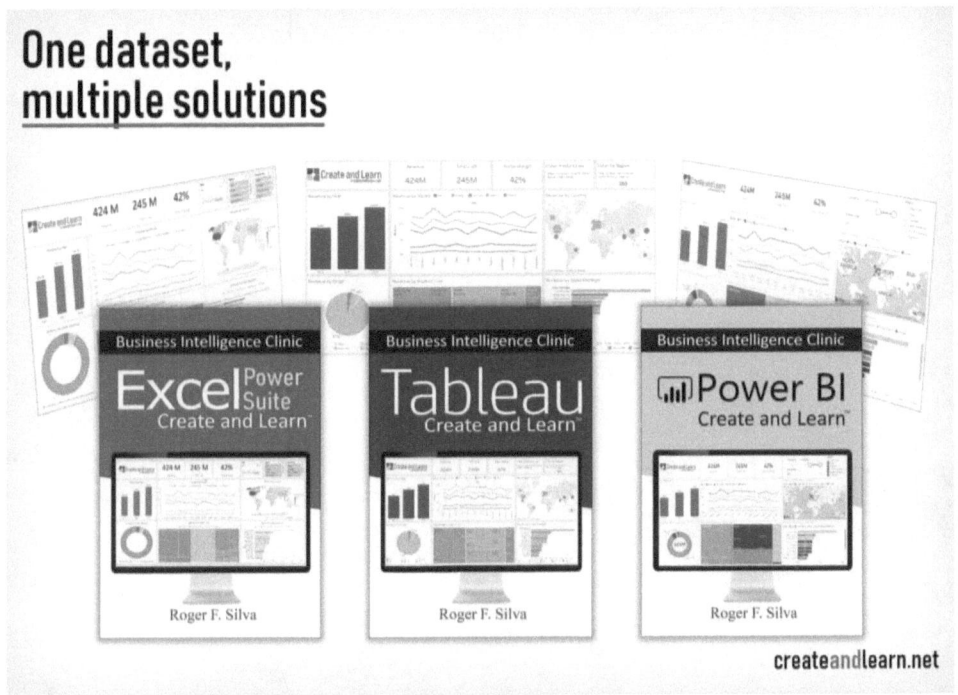

www.ingramcontent.com/pod-product-compliance
Lightning Source LLC
Chambersburg PA
CBHW032009170526
45157CB00002B/621